Bello
hidden talent rediscovered

Bello is a digital-only imprint of Pan Macmillan,
established to breathe new life into previously published,
classic books.

At Bello we believe in the timeless power of the imagination,
of a good story, narrative and entertainment, and we want to
use digital technology to ensure that many more readers
can enjoy these books into the future.

We publish in ebook and print-on-demand formats
to bring these wonderful books to new audiences.

www.panmacmillan.com/imprint-publishers/bello

Robert Rhodes James

Sir Robert Rhodes James (1933-1999) was a British historian, biographer and Member of Parliament. He published his first book – a biography of Lord Randolph Churchill – in 1959 and went on to write many other highly acclaimed biographies of political and royal figures. His subjects included King George VI, Anthony Eden, Prince Albert, Winston Churchill and Lord Rosebery, the last of which won him the Royal Society's Literary Award. His second book, *An Introduction to the House of Commons*, won the 1962 John Llewelyn Rhys Prize.

Robert Rhodes James

AN INTRODUCTION
TO THE
HOUSE OF COMMONS

BELL◎

First published in 1961 by Collins

This edition published 2017 by Bello
an imprint of Pan Macmillan
20 New Wharf Road, London N1 9RR
Associated companies throughout the world

www.panmacmillan.com/imprint-publishers/bello

ISBN 978-1-5098-5891-0 EPUB
ISBN 978-1-5098-5890-3 PB

A CIP catalogue record for this book is available from the British Library.

Typeset by Ellipsis Digital Limited, Glasgow

Visit **www.panmacmillan.com** to read more about all our books
and to buy them. You will also find features, author interviews and
news of any author events, and you can sign up for e-newsletters
so that you're always first to hear about our new releases.

To the A.P.s, with love

Contents

Preface

Innumerable books have been written on the subject of the British Parliament, but although there are many excellent histories of Parliament and numerous text-books on procedure, there are at the moment very few books—if any—which briefly describe not what *was* done, or *should* be done, but what *is* done to-day. My endeavour is to provide a photograph, as it were, of the House of Commons to-day; to describe what happens, and why it happens, and to convey an accurate portrait of the processes of Parliament to the general reader.

I have limited my survey to the House of Commons, which is the third partner in the triumvirate—the Sovereign, the Lords, and the Commons—which, together, form the British Parliament. For one thing, the subject of Parliament is so vast that it is not easy to provide an accurate and brief account of it; for another, I am not qualified to write on the subject of the House of Lords; and, finally, the House of Commons is the true seat of power and—except on rare occasions—the centre of public interest.

So much of what the House of Commons does to-day is linked to what happened in the past that it is impossible to avoid the occasional backward glance. I have therefore described in some detail how the actual Chamber of the House has evolved, since an understanding of this is essential if one is to realise how the House functions to-day.

It is not an easy task to describe the complicated machinery of the House in simple terms without actually misleading the reader. I have tried to reduce all technical words and phrases to a minimum, but as this is not always possible I have included a brief Glossary of Parliamentary Terms at the end of the book, and I hope that the reader will not be irritated by my exhortations to consult it on occasions. I have also added a list of books recommended for future reading for those who wish to plunge deeper into the subject.

Although the work and procedure of the House seem to become more complicated every year—a chapter which I wrote for this book on procedure at the beginning of the Parliamentary Session of 1959–60 was already out of date in several respects by the end of that Session—the curious feature of the House of Commons is really how very little it has changed down the years. "In my time," the late Joseph Chamberlain remarked over fifty years ago, "I have never known the House of Commons without a funny man. Then there is the House of Commons bore—of course there is more than one, but there is always one *par excellence*; he is generally a man of encyclopaedic information which he has been unable to digest himself and which, therefore, he is always ready to impart to everybody else. Then you have the weighty man, and the gravity of the weighty man of the House of Commons is a thing to which there is no parallel in the world. You have the foolish man, you have the man with one idea, you have the independent man, you have the man who is a little cracked." A Member of the eighteenth or twentieth centuries would have little difficulty in recognising these characters.

The House of Commons is essentially a human institution, and, as such, it has its bad periods and its good; does stupid things and wise ones; its mood can change bewilderingly from day to day, and even from hour to hour. It is indeed this fickleness which provides so much of its curious and undefinable charm. When the aged Wilberforce was told by a young lady that her brother was to enter the House the old man said warmly, "Ah! I hear that shout again—'Hear, hear!' What a life it was!" "I have tried all forms of excitement," Lord Randolph Churchill—father of Sir Winston— once remarked, "from tip-cat to tiger-shooting; all degrees of gambling, from beggar-my-neighbour to Monte Carlo; but have found no gambling like politics, and no excitement like a big division in the House of Commons."

It is the portrait of this unique, inconstant, demanding and fascinating place that I have attempted to trace in this book, and I should like to express my gratitude to those friends and colleagues who have so generously assisted me in my task of presenting this Introduction to the House of Commons.

ROBERT RHODES JAMES

Priory Close,
Cartmel,
North Lancashire
April, 1961

CHAPTER ONE

The Power of the Commons

The history of England since the end of the thirteenth century has witnessed the remorseless advance of the House of Commons from a position of being the least influential to the most important single element in the British Parliament. "Parliament" is the meeting of the Sovereign, the Lords and the Commons, and the House of Commons—so-called because they represented the *communes*, or communities, and not the lower classes—obtained their supremacy over the Sovereign and the Lords principally by their control over the nation's money. The establishment of the principle that the remedy of grievance must come before the granting of money to the Government is the most important single factor in the story of the rise of the Commons.

The Chancellor of the Exchequer proposes to the House early in the year—usually at the beginning of April—in his "Budget Statement," that certain taxes will be imposed upon the people to provide the nation's income. His proposals have to be agreed to that day by the Committee of Ways and Means to which he makes the statement, and the new taxes can be imposed at once; they are then put into legislative form in the Finance Bill, which must go through Parliament within four months, or the taxes will lapse. The national housekeeping money is paid to Government Departments out of what is called the Consolidated Fund. This is a banking account into which all taxes and other revenues of the country are paid, and out of which all government expenditure is made. These payments are made by the authority of other Acts of Parliament, and the Government Departments have to present accounts showing exactly how they have spent the money voted to them by Parliament. Although the House of Lords can reject a "money" Bill passed by the Commons, the Bill can receive the Royal Assent without the consent of the Lords,[1] so it will be seen that the control of the nation's finances lies in the hands of the lower House although the Lords may make suggestions.

This power, the greatest of all possessed by the House of Commons, is surrounded with certain limitations; no legislation involving the expenditure of public money can be entered upon unless the Queen's Recommendation has been signified to the House by a Minister of the Crown, and this means in practice that only the Government can present proposals for public finance, although the Commons can *reduce*—but not increase—the amount of money requested. The House votes money for one year only, specifies what it must be used for, and any left over at the end of that year must normally be returned to the Exchequer. The Government presents its annual *Estimates*—its forecast of the amount of money needed to run the country for the forthcoming year—early each year, and these Estimates are broken down into Classes (dealing with groups of Departments) and further into Votes, which set out in greater detail how the money is going to be spent. These Estimates go before the Committee of Supply for their agreement, and after the House has consented to the report of this Committee, the Committee of Ways and Means authorises the expenditure out of the Consolidated Fund, and the House passes the Consolidated Fund (Appropriation) Bill which sets the legislative seal on the whole process. The Commons not only vote the money to the Government; they also set up various Select Committees[2] to see that it is spent properly.

Great Britain is ruled by "Her Majesty's Government." In theory, the Queen could invite anyone she wished to become her Prime

---

1 As a result of the Parliament Act of 1911. The Lords had rejected the Finance Bill of 1909, and the Parliament Act was the result of a long and bitter controversy between the two political parties and both Houses.
2 See Chapter Eight.

2

Minister and form a Government, but in fact she invites the Leader of the political party in the House of Commons which commands the support of a majority of its Members. Most of the Ministers in the Government are Members of the House of Commons, answerable to that House for their actions and policies. If the Commons withdraw their confidence from a Government it could no longer serve Her Majesty, as it could not guarantee the passing of legislation nor the granting of the money necessary for the administration of the country. The Commons are, therefore, in the position of *controlling* the Government without actually *being* the Government. Their principal duties are to advise, criticise, and supervise.

The second largest collection of Members of the House form "Her Majesty's Opposition," and their Leader has a salary from the Consolidated Fund. This body of men and women is in effect the alternative Government, prepared to form an Administration when it has a majority of Members in the House; it is guided by a "Shadow Cabinet," composed of persons who are likely to hold office when their party has a majority in the House and forms the Government. "The function of an Opposition is to oppose, and not to support, the Government," Lord Randolph Churchill once declared, but the conduct of the Opposition differs wildly under different circumstances. There have been many occasions when the gap between the Government and Opposition has seemed to be very small, and there have been others when deep emotions of mutual distrust and animosity have poisoned the atmosphere of the House. A good Opposition is alert and critical of the Government, but not merely hostile for the sake of hostility.

The House has secured certain privileges for itself and its Members which are, in effect, powers. It has the right to provide for its own composition in that it can issue writs for by-elections to fill vacancies caused by the death or resignation[1] of Members, and it is the judge

---

1 A Member may not resign his seat in the course of a Parliament, but can apply for the title of "Steward of the Chiltern Hundreds", or, if that post is filled, as "Steward of the Manor of Northstead". His request is always accepted, and his appointment means that he has accepted "an office of profit under the Crown"—although the duties are negligible—and thereby automatically vacates his seat.

of whether Members are qualified to sit in the House. It has complete control over its own affairs and procedure, and can expel or suspend Members who offend against its rules, and can imprison, fine, or severely reprimand persons who infringe its Privileges or treat it with contempt. But the House does not interfere with the course of justice in the Law Courts, nor does the Government, and this is an important voluntary limitation to the powers of the House. If a matter is *sub judice*, in other words, before the Law Courts, the House does not debate it.

The powers of the Commons do not rest solely upon written laws: they principally repose in unwritten laws of convention, and it is when these conventions are defied—as happened when the Lords rejected the Finance Bill (the Budget) in 1909—that the Commons turn to legislation to establish their rights. There is no law, for example, which says that the Prime Minister must be a Member of the House of Commons, but there has not been one outside it since Lord Salisbury resigned in 1902, and it is very difficult to imagine that there will ever be another.

It is by persuasion and criticism, as much as by Resolutions, Bills, or Divisions, that the Commons affect the administration of the country. What is called "the mood of the House" can be a very important factor. A Minister may find himself under hot fire from Members on both sides of the House on a particular matter, either at Question Time or in debate, and the House can make life extremely unpleasant for a Minister who, it feels, is not "coming clean." The tone of the questioners becomes distinctly less polite, the growls of the discontented Members grow in volume until the dreaded chant "Resign!" is heard, while the hapless recipient of this anger is assailed with interjections when he tries to reply. A Minister who cannot handle this kind of situation in the House stands little chance of keeping his job for very long. His supporters, sitting behind him in serried ranks, will not relish the spectacle of one of their leaders being crushed in argument, and he will be written down as a liability. "He was tried in the fire and was found wanting" is not an uncommon epitaph on an unsuccessful Ministerial career. A grim silence from his own supporters can be as eloquent as actual opposition to a Minister in difficulties at the Dispatch Box. A Minister was once asked if he appreciated the silent hostility of his supporters—sitting, of course, behind him—to a statement he had made in the House; "I could feel it through the back of my neck," he replied. A wise Minister will reserve his appeals to his colleagues for really important matters; on subjects of lesser importance, a graceful concession at an early stage is usually preferable to an unnecessary and damaging Parliamentary storm. The House of Commons can be terrifyingly cruel when angered, and this occasional harshness is calculated to keep Ministers on their toes and make them wary of offending the House.

If the Government is determined on a particular course, and can secure their full majority in the House, the Opposition can only hope to delay the inevitable. "Majorities must rule, but minorities have their rights," is the unwritten law of the British democracy, and the Government which tries to bludgeon the House of Commons or treat it with contempt would court disaster. People tend to exaggerate the effect of Party control on backbench Members of Parliament; the House of Commons has a very strong collective spirit, and is as proud as the devil.

The great power which the Commons has over the Government is that the Minister who makes the decision has to come to the Dispatch Box and explain his reasons. He can then be questioned by Members, praised, criticised or attacked; a Motion of Censure on his decision, can be "tabled" by the Opposition, and, by convention, must be debated as soon as possible. The Minister represents a large Department of many Civil Servants, who cannot be questioned about their conduct by Parliament on matters of policy, but the Minister can; he is responsible for all the acts of his Department, even if he had no knowledge of some of them. The villagers of Little Middling ask for a Post Office; the officials at the Ministry say that they cannot have one, as they have a perfectly good Post Office five miles away at Greater Middling. The Member in whose constituency the village lies is asked to raise the matter in the House; he puts down a Question, and the

Postmaster-General asks his officials for the details of the controversy. If they have made a serious mistake, and have put the Minister in the wrong, he must take the responsibility. He can issue a severe reprimand to the officials privately, but in the eyes of the House of Commons he is the man responsible; any attempt to shuffle off this responsibility on to his Civil Servants would infuriate the House. Civil Servants who are incompetent or who place the Minister in an impossible position in the House can be persuaded to resign or are removed to positions of less importance, but it must be made absolutely clear that it is the Minister who is responsible to the House of Commons for the errors of his officials. In 1954 there occurred what was popularly called the Crichel Down Case, when it was discovered that certain officials of the Ministry of Agriculture had behaved in a particularly disagreeable manner over some land in Dorset. The Minister was closely questioned in the House, and after an Inquiry had been held, which strongly criticised the officials, it was the Minister who resigned, as the man responsible for the sins of his Ministry.

The House of Commons possesses another power, which is not usually appreciated. The Prime Minister chooses his own Ministers, some of whom have to be in the House of Lords, but of whom the majority are in the Commons. To be a Minister, therefore, it is essential for all but a very few people to be Members of the House of Commons, and to have made their impact upon the House. However influential a man may be within his own party, it is on the floor of the House that he must prove himself. It is the most competitive place on earth, and, being comparatively small, men eye each other with such narrowness that exceptional qualities of perseverance, application, ability and courage are demanded. The history of the House of Commons is littered with the relics of promising careers which have been destroyed under the concentrated parliamentary arc-light. The silver-tongued street-corner orator, the brilliant but shifty lawyer, the skilful and ambitious party politician, the pompous and opinionated successful business-man, the self-satisfied and long-winded ex-Lord Mayor, all are cut down to size. A fine reputation outside Westminster can be a positive disadvantage, for the House has its own standards, and by them everyone is mercilessly judged. In a curious, roundabout manner, this is one of the greatest powers of the House of Commons—that of discovering and discarding the charlatan, so that he will never be in a position to control the destinies of the country.

The growth of party organisation in the House of Commons in the last hundred years is an example of the fact that the Commons is the seat of power. Men and women group themselves together in political parties to achieve certain objects. They do not necessarily agree upon everything, but they are united on certain basic principles. The House of Commons is the stage on which the struggle for power is waged between these contending factions. Inevitably, there are individuals on the fringes of every political party who have few deep feelings on principles but who are intent solely upon their own careers; the party is a vehicle for their ambitions, and provides them with the opportunity of power. There are also those people who despise political slanging matches and who are public servants in the very highest sense of the phrase.

The vital importance of organising his followers into a coherent group was first appreciated in the modern sense by the Irish leader, Charles Stewart Parnell, in the late 1870's and 1880's. He ruled his Irish Home Rule party with a rod of iron, and those Members who did not accept his leadership were ruthlessly rejected by the Irish electorate. By 1885 the Parnellite "label" was indispensable for any Irish Nationalist who wished to enter the House of Commons *and stay there.*

The party system is now a firmly entrenched feature of the life of the House of Commons. In return for the support of the individual Member, the party assists him in a variety of ways, from paying for his election expenses to providing him with research facilities. The party will tolerate the occasional defection and difference of opinion, but will not—and, indeed, cannot—allow a Member who is causing damage to it to remain under the party "umbrella." The power which the party possesses is, therefore, very great. If it withdraws its support from a Member, this will almost certainly lead to his political extinction; so far as the House of Commons is concerned, he will simply disappear at the next election, and, as Disraeli once remarked with laconic truth, "The first requisite for success in the House of Commons is to be there." The party does not have to resort to extreme measures very often, for the rules are well understood by Members, who shape their conduct accordingly.

It is often said that the party system weakens the power of the Commons: it has certainly reduced the freedom of Members, but it is difficult to see how it affects the *power* of the Commons. Indeed, the fact that the Opposition can co-ordinate its actions and provide facilities for research is a very definite element in the Commons' role of supervising, advising, and criticising the Government, which has all the facilities of the Civil Service behind it.

Without the confidence and support of the House of Commons the Government of the country could not be carried on; this is the measure of the strength of the powers of the Commons. They control finance, in that they must approve it; their assent is required for legislation; they demand the right to insist that the men who make policy should defend it to them. The House of Commons is not a debating society; it is the seat of power. "Parliament," the late Lord Birkenhead once said, "is the microcosm of the talent of Great Britain; and no man conscious of great powers should ever, willingly, be excluded from it."

CHAPTER TWO

The Chamber of the House

There has been a Royal Palace at Westminster since the reign of King Edward the Confessor. The outstanding features of the old palace were Westminster Hall, begun in the eleventh century in the reign of William II, and St. Stephen's Chapel, founded by Edward I and completed about 1350. Whereas Westminster Hall was massy, impressive, and gloomy, St. Stephen's—which was built at a right angle to the Hall, facing the River Thames—was tall, airy, delicate, and most richly ornamented. It was about ninety feet long, thirty feet wide inside, and over ninety feet tall, and was built on two floors. On the ground floor the servants and attendants of the Court worshipped, while the King and his more important courtiers used the main chapel above it. Around the stolid Westminster Hall and the lofty St. Stephen's there clustered an extraordinary variety of buildings, some beautiful, some mean, in which were housed the offices of the central government and the law courts. By the reign of Henry VIII the machinery of government had long outgrown the conglomeration of ill-assorted buildings which huddled round the Hall and Chapel and fringed the unbanked and fast-flowing Thames, and much of it was removed to Whitehall Palace.

Since the Commons had first begun to grow in importance in the fourteenth century they had held their meetings in various places near, and at times in, the Palace of Westminster. In 1341— when St. Stephen's was nearing completion—they met in the Painted

Chamber, which was a small room to the south of Westminster Hall, and in 1352 they occupied the Chapter House of the Abbey for their deliberations. In 1368 they are discovered in the Little Hall, another chamber in the Palace, but in 1376 the Chapter House is described as "their former place," and they appear to have met here until 1395, when they moved to the Refectory of the Abbey for twenty years or so, and then there occurs a complete gap in our records.

It is probable that the Commons had been agitating for their own home for some time when Henry VIII's reign closed, for they were exercising a steadily increasing influence, of which they were not unconscious. In 1547 it was decided to accede to their requests, and the Protector Somerset, who ruled in the minority of the youthful Edward VI, handed over St. Stephen's Chapel to the Commons for their use. This decision to house a secular assembly in a consecrated chapel was in the spirit of post-Reformation England, and St. Stephen's itself had lain deserted for several years, with no services conducted and with its once considerable wealth confiscated. From this decision, which may have stemmed partly from expediency and partly from malice, the history of the modern House of Commons may be said to begin.

The Commons entered the upper chapel to find that it was still set up as a chapel, with choir-stalls on either side and the altar at the head of the altar steps beneath a large east window. The choir was divided from a small ante-chapel by a carved wooden screen, which had a door in the middle. The Members sat in the choir-stalls, looking across the floor at each other, they removed the altar and put the Speaker's chair in its place, they put a table and chair for the Clerk at the foot of the altar steps, and they called the ante-chapel the Lobby. The visitor looking down from the galleries on to the present House of Commons is regarding an extension and enlargement of the arrangements discovered by the Members in 1547 when they took possession of the upper chapel of St. Stephen's. An account by an eyewitness of the House in 1571 reveals how little it has changed down the centuries.

This House is framed and made like unto a theatre, being four rows of seats one above another, round about the House. At the higher end, in the middle of the lowest row, is a seat made for the Speaker, where he is appointed to sit; and before him sitteth the Clerk of the House, having a little board before him to write and lay his books upon. Upon the lower row, next to the Speaker, sit all such of Queen's Privy Council and head officers as be knights or burgesses for that House; but after, everyone sitteth as he cometh, no difference being there held of any degree, because each man in that place is of like calling.

As the years passed the chapel went through many alterations. The choir-stalls were replaced by benches, which also ran behind the Speaker's Chair so that when the House was full the Speaker seemed to rise out of a lapping sea of faces; the beautiful paintings and statues were covered with tapestries, and in some cases were actually defaced; at some time in the early part of the seventeenth century the roof was lowered, and the large east window went through a series of "improvements." But the basic structure of the House was unaltered; the Chamber was astonishingly small—sixty feet long and thirty feet wide—and was reached through Westminster Hall and up a staircase which led into the Lobby.

The seventeenth century witnessed the decisive emergence of the House of Commons to its position of eminence over the Sovereign and the Lords, and throughout the tangled and dramatic events of the century one must envisage the narrow inconvenient little chapel where rested the new repository of power in the land. It was in this chapel that the Grand Remonstrance was passed by one vote after a tense and harsh debate; it was to this place that Charles I and his soldiers came in 1642 to demand the five Members who had incurred his wrath, and where Cromwell brought his troops to clear the House and summarily end the "Rump" Parliament.

St. Stephen's Chapel was virtually the only facility possessed by the House, as the Palace of Westminster contained many of the various courts of law—and continued to do so until the middle of the nineteenth century—and other offices of the executive government, and in the reign of Queen Elizabeth a host of private houses, shops, taverns, ale-houses and small, unhealthy alleyways sprang up and added to the already considerable congestion round the great Hall and St. Stephen's. Towards the end of the seventeenth century a determined attempt was made to improve conditions in the House itself, which was bitterly cold in winter, suffocatingly hot in summer, and dreadfully overcrowded whenever an important debate was in progress. Sir Christopher Wren, then Surveyor-General of His Majesty's Works, supervised the changes, which consisted of a further lowering of the ceiling, the provision of narrow galleries running along each side of the chapel and one facing the Speaker's Chair, the covering of the stone walls with wooden panelling, and another alteration of the east window, this time into three graceful rounded windows. A narrow gallery outside the chapel behind the Speaker's Chair was also built, and it was in this passage that the younger Pitt, recovering from an excess of port, once vomited, while holding the door into the House open so that be could hear the speech of Charles James Fox. A visitor to England towards the end of the eighteenth century came to St. Stephen's and recorded his impressions.

I now, for the first time saw the whole of the British nation assembled in its representatives, in a rather mean-looking building that not a little resembles a chapel. The Speaker, an elderly man dressed in an enormous wig with two knotted curls behind and a black cloak, with a hat on his head,[1] sat opposite me on a lofty chair. The Members have nothing particular in their dress. They even come into the House in their great-coats and with boots and spurs. It is not at all uncommon to see a member lying stretched out on one of the benches while others are debating; some crack nuts, others eat oranges or whatever else is in season. Two shorthand writers sat not far from me, who endeavoured to take down the words

1 The Speaker no longer wears his hat—a black three-cornered one, in a style common in the eighteenth century—but it is at hand in the House, and he uses it formally to deliver a reprimand to persons who have incurred the displeasure of the House.

of the speakers; and thus all that is very remarkable may generally be read in print next day.

Wren's alterations did little to affect the principal defect of St. Stephen's, which was that it was itself far too small and that the offices of the House were woefully inadequate. The Act of Union of 1800, which sent over a hundred Irish Members to Westminster, made the problem even more acute. It was partly solved by knocking down the thick walls between the pillars of the old chapel, replacing them with thinner ones, and thus achieving an increase of seats. But this ingenious plan barely touched the real problem. For an example of the wretchedly inadequate accommodation available to Members, there were only two committee rooms over the cloisters of the chapel, each of which was twenty feet square and could only be reached by a narrow spiral staircase. Until the 1790's the Clerks had virtually no space for their records and papers, and the Commons did not have a library of any kind until 1818. Three schemes for the complete rebuilding of the accommodation of the House were prepared (in 1735 and 1739 by William Kent, and in 1793 by Sir John Soane) but nothing was done. Although rooms for the Speaker, the Clerks and the Serjeant at Arms were provided in the 1790's, the situation was still so desperate that in 1801 Hatsell, the Clerk of the House, wrote, "But all these great manœuvres I leave, as I do matters of higher import, to the Gods, who *must* make Peace, or continue the war, and *must* find a new set of Committee Rooms." The few improvements effected left the House and its offices unhealthily cramped, insanitary and grossly overcrowded. "Why are we squeezed into so small a space that it is absolutely impossible that there should be calm and regular discussion, even from that circumstance alone?" William Cobbett demanded in 1833. "Why do we live in this hubbub? Why are we exposed to all these inconveniences? Why are 658 of us crammed into a space that allows to each of us no more than a foot and a half square, while, at the same time, each of the servants of the King, whom we pay, has a palace to live in, and more unoccupied space in that palace than the little hole into which we are all crammed to make the laws by which this great kingdom is governed?" A journalist was struck by the same fact.

I shall not soon forget the disappointment which I experienced on the first sight of the interior of the House of Commons. I had been told that it but ill accorded with the dignity of what has been termed the first assembly of gentlemen in the world, or with the importance of the subjects on which they were convened to legislate. But I was not at all prepared for such a place as I then beheld. It was dark, gloomy, and badly ventilated, and so small that no more than four hundred out of the six hundred and fifty-eight members could be accommodated in it with any measure of comfort. When an important debate occurred . . . the members were really to be pitied; they were literally crammed together, and the heat of the house rendered it in some degree a second edition of the Black Hole of Calcutta. On either side there was a gallery, every corner of which was occupied by legislators; and many, not being able to get even standing room, were obliged to lounge in the refreshment apartments adjoining St. Stephen's, until the division—when they rushed to the voting room in as much haste as if the place they had quitted had been on fire.[1]

The accommodation provided for visitors was no better, consisting of a few benches in the gallery facing the Speaker, and they could only use this cramped space if they had an order signed by a Member or if they gave the doorkeeper half-a-crown. Press reporters had the back bench in the gallery reserved for them, and paid three guineas a session for this privilege to the doorkeeper. Women were not allowed into the galleries at all; this arose from an incident in 1778 when a Member called attention to the presence of Strangers; the galleries were ordered to be cleared, but several women refused to leave, and held up the business of the House for nearly two hours before they were removed. The ban against women was so severe after this incident that even wives of Members

---

1 Grant: *Random Recollections of the House of Commons.*

had to disguise themselves as men to enter the galleries—Sheridan's wife was one who did this—or they were allowed to go into the garret over the Chamber and peer down through the hole which was cut in the roof of the House to let the fumes escape from the large chandelier. "The smoke of the candles, and the heated atmosphere they inhaled, combined with the awkwardness of the position they were obliged to assume, made the situation so very unpleasant that few remained long in it," Grant has recorded. "Those only who were anxious to hear their husbands, or brothers, or lovers, make some expected oration, had the fortitude to endure the semi-martyrdom of remaining many minutes in such a place."

The smallness of the Chamber had one conspicuous merit: it was ideal for the purposes of debate. It also made for emotion, since passions could easily arise in such a small room where there were any number of Members present, wedged in their benches, or massed at the Bar, facing the Speaker. This feature has never been lost, for the House of Commons has always been a highly emotional place, where tempers can be lost very quickly and where storms can arise out of complete calm in a matter of moments.

Since the middle of the eighteenth century experts had been pointing out the very serious danger of fire in the Palace. A Select Committee of the House in 1789 painted a horrifying—and, as it turned out, very accurate—picture of these dangers from the proximity to the House and Westminster Hall of so many ancient timber and brick buildings. In 1828 Sir John Soane repeated the warning, again unheeded. "In such an extensive assemblage of combustible materials, should a fire happen, what would become of the Painted Chamber, the House of Commons, and Westminster Hall?" he wrote. "Where would the progress of the fire be arrested? The want of security from fire, the narrow, gloomy and unhealthy passages, and the insufficiency of the accommodations in this building, are important subjects which call loudly for revision and speedy amendment." On the night of 16th October, 1834, the inevitable occurred, and the Chamber which had housed the Commons for nearly three hundred years was gutted by a great fire which destroyed or mortally damaged most of the old Palace.

The fire started in the heating system of the House of Lords, where old wooden Exchequer "tallies"—pieces of wood notched and used as receipts until 1826—were used too enthusiastically for the boilers. Visitors to the House of Lords that afternoon complained of the heat, and said afterwards that they could feel the heat of the floor through their shoes and could hardly see across the House for the smoke. Later in the evening it was realised that the building was on fire, and the Clerk of the Works in the Department of Woods and Forests—who was responsible for the idea of using the tallies for fuel—saw a chimney "very much on fire" and raised the alarm. But by then it was too late to do anything except try and save those parts of the Palace which were some distance from the seat of the fire, particularly Westminster Hall. The flames, now in complete control, were fanned by a brisk wind. The scene was one of lurid grandeur, and all London turned out to see the excitement. "The moon was near the full and shone with radiance," wrote a spectator. "But occasionally vast masses of cumulus clouds floated high and bright across the skies, and as the fitful glare of the flames increased, were illumined in a remarkably impressive manner . . . Even the River Thames, in the vicinity of the spot, was covered with boats and barges full of persons whom curiosity had attracted to the scene; and the reflections of the wavering flames upon the water, on the neighbouring shores, and on the many thousands thus congregated, composed a spectacle most strikingly picturesque and impressive." When dawn came on 17th October, St. Stephen's Chapel, like most of the Palace—except Westminster Hall, which was virtually undamaged—was a smoking ruin. The Commons moved into the House of Lords which had, surprisingly enough, survived the fire, while the Lords found temporary refuge in the Painted Chamber.

The orange glow which covered London on the night of 16th October was seen by the occupants of a coach returning from Brighton, one of whom was Charles Barry, then thirty-nine years of age, a successful, ambitious and energetic architect. Having witnessed the destruction of most of the old Palace with a barely-concealed exultation, he called upon Mr. Augustus Welby Pugin on the morning of the following day. Pugin was then twenty-two, and was already well known as a passionate and expert advocate of the Gothic revival in English architecture. Pugin set to work at once upon preparing plans for the new Palace which Barry had foreseen must be built, and when a competition was held some months later, the design submitted by Barry and Pugin was accepted. Bitter controversy later arose as to who actually was the master-mind behind the design, and the question can probably never be resolved, but it seems to be the case that Pugin provided the inspiration and the exquisite plans while to Barry must go most of the credit for the basic design. What is apparent is that neither of these curiously diverse men could have by himself produced the finished building. The industrious, ambitious, stolid and not over-scrupulous Barry and the brilliant, selfless but erratic Pugin, made a remarkable combination, and it is fair that all credit and blame for the new Palace which arose out of the ruins of the old must be shared by both.

The new Palace covers some eight acres, with the Clock Tower, known throughout the world as "Big Ben", at the north-east corner and the square Victoria Tower at the southern end. Between these two conspicuous towers there straggles one of the most extraordinary buildings in the world, with its curious little towers, Gothic windows and exquisitely carved but almost invisible detail, carefully copied from medieval originals. The Palace is linked with numerous little courtyards, so that it is possible to drive into New Palace Yard at the north-west corner, go through Speaker's Court, and southwards through the whole length of the building as far as the Victoria Tower and out into the main road again. Broadly speaking, the Commons occupy the northern half of the Palace, and the Lords the southern, and the central point is a large circular hall, covered by a dome, and which is known as the Central Lobby. It is here that constituents wait to see their Members, and it is usually crowded when Parliament is in session, with visitors—always called "Strangers"—Members, Peers, their guests and friends, and hurrying officials and messengers. If one stands in the middle of the hall and looks to the north, one can see the short corridor leading to the Members' Lobby, the Lobby itself, and through it to the House; to the south there is a similar corridor, the Lords' Lobby, and the House of Lords itself. When the Queen is on the Throne in the Lords, and all the doors are thrown open, she can see the Speaker in his Chair. The Palace of Westminster is the property of the Queen, and its affairs are managed by the Lord Great Chamberlain on her behalf.

The upper chapel of St. Stephen's was beyond repair, but the lower chapel—used at one time by the Speaker for a dining-room—had survived the fire, and was eventually restored as a chapel. Barry used the site of the old House as a corridor, retaining the original dimensions, so that visitors can to-day realise just how small is a room thirty feet by sixty as a deliberative chamber for over six hundred men. In the new Palace the House of Commons was given facilities which were commodious and magnificent. Committee Rooms were provided in far greater numbers than had ever been available before, and a splendid set of rooms for the Library was provided.

The new Chamber of the House, although considerably larger than St. Stephen's, was still small, providing seating accommodation for only 346 Members. The arrangements and proportions of the old House were retained, and the tall stained-glass windows and dark, richly carved wood-work continued—perhaps rather self-consciously—the "chapel" atmosphere. The historic antipathy towards women "strangers" was continued, and a gallery was provided for their use high above the Press Gallery behind the Speaker's Chair, and was covered with a wire grille! There was some pressure upon the architects to abandon the oblong shape of the old House by Members and even, it has been alleged, by the Government, but Barry accepted the strong advice of the officials of the House that what was needed was an enlarged St. Stephen's, and this is what resulted.

When Members took possession of their new home in 1852 they were highly displeased. Having used the considerably larger House of Lords for several years they disliked returning to the cramped confines of Barry's House. They complained vociferously about the acoustics, and Barry was ordered to lower the ceiling; although the Lords was a larger chamber, it had been fitted with a low glass ceiling which, the Members believed, improved the acoustics. Barry, after passionate but unavailing protests, complied with the order, and the gorgeously carved wooden roof and most of the tall stained-glass windows disappeared for ever behind a glass-panelled ceiling. Barry felt so deeply about this mutilation that he refused to enter the Chamber except when compelled to do so, and he never mentioned the subject again.

Although the acoustics were wonderfully improved by the new roof, the smallness of the Chamber continued to irritate Members, and in 1867 a Select Committee of the House was set up to look into the matter, and reported that "the present House of Commons is defective in the necessary extent of accommodation." Barry, worn out as much by the interminable wranglings as by the vast amount of work which surrounded his task, was dead, but his son was commissioned to draw up plans for a new House of Commons, which he presented in 1868.

His proposals were completely revolutionary; he planned to build a magnificent new Chamber in Commons Court—which runs parallel to the Chamber on the eastern side—using the old House with the obnoxious glass ceiling removed, as a Lobby. The new House of Commons was to be square, and would seat 559 Members in comfort and 600 on important occasions. The scheme was warmly applauded, and there is little doubt that it would have been carried into effect had not there occurred a General Election which displaced Disraeli's Conservative Government and installed Gladstone with a large Liberal majority possessed of a formidable and contentious legislative programme of Reform. The proposal for building the new House gradually died away, and within a few years was almost completely forgotten. It has also vanished from the official history of the Palace of Westminster, and only the faded copies of the plans and the yellowing reports of the Select Committee bear witness to the revolution that so very nearly came to pass.

Barry's House was used by the Commons until 10th May, 1941, when the German bombs plucked it out of the Palace of Westminster with such neatness that the corridors leading to it were virtually unharmed, although the Members' Lobby was wrecked. As in 1834, the main effort of the fire-fighters was devoted to saving Westminster Hall, and the room which had witnessed every major political controversy since 1852 was completely gutted. The Commons, with the exception of a hapless interlude in Church House, Westminster, again took over the House of Lords, and within a short time, partly as a gesture of defiance, plans for a new House on the site of the old were being discussed. Mr. Churchill (as he then was) was the most powerful advocate of what was virtually a replica of Barry's House of Commons, and in proposing the motion for a select committee in October 1943 he strongly supported the proportions of the old arrangement.

> If the House is big enough to contain all its Members, nine-tenths of the Debates will be conducted in the depressing atmosphere of an almost empty or half-empty Chamber. The essence of good House of Commons speaking is the conversational style, the facility for quick, informal interruptions and interchanges. Harangues from a rostrum would be a bad substitute for the conversational style in which so much of our business is done. But the conversational style requires a fairly small space, and there should be on great occasions a sense of crowd and urgency. There should be a sense of the importance of much that is said and a sense that great matters are being declared, there and then, by the House.

Although much that Mr. Churchill said in the course of that famous speech about the importance of the size and shape of the House can be strongly disputed—particularly the suggestion that the arrangement of the benches has led to the two-party system—there is no doubt that his argument was basically correct. The smallness of the House of Commons has never had any influence on the form of debate, and the "conversational style" is a comparatively modern development, there being fashions in oratory as well as in everything else. The smallness of St. Stephen's did not inhibit Pitt, Fox or Sheridan from speaking very loudly, and delivering set orations lasting for several hours: Macaulay has described how the elder Pitt's voice "rose like the swell of an organ of a great cathedral, shook the House with its peal, and was heard through lobbies and down staircases to the Court of Requests and the precincts of Westminster Hall." But to all who know the House of Commons, how wonderfully evocative is Churchill's phrase "a sense of crowd and urgency!" The packed benches and galleries, the Members crouched in the gangways, massing round the Speaker's Chair, the phalanx at the Bar, the almost tangible tension which manifests itself in gusts of excessive laughter at the most laboured jokes as the critical moment draws near, and then the tense and dangerous quietness, which can be changed into unbelievable tumult by a single injudicious phrase. Thus was the House crammed for the debate on the Grand Remonstrance in 1641, or for the elder Pitt's great orations, or for the debate on the first Reform Bill in 1831, right down to the crowded and harsh debates on the Suez crisis in 1956, creating a bond which links the present Member with his predecessor of hundreds of years ago. Nowadays, when so much complicated business is dealt with on the Floor of the House, particularly in Committee, there is no time for the great speech lasting several hours, and the conversational style necessitates a reasonably small House of Commons.

The present Chamber, designed by Sir Giles Gilbert Scott, is almost a replica of Barry's House, although considerably lighter and less ornamented. The most noticeable differences are the wooden roof, the lighter colour of the oak used for the panelling, and the size of the galleries, which, by an ingenious stratagem of the architect go back beyond the walls of the Chamber at the ends facing and standing behind the Speaker's Chair. The dimensions of the Floor of the House are almost exactly the same, and the seating arrangements discovered in St. Stephen's in 1547 are faithfully maintained. The tradition that Members should be critical has been continued, for it was discovered that the acoustics were not nearly so good as in Barry's House, some Members were distressed by the rather grey and anaemic oak, others disliked the fluorescent lighting in the ceiling, and for a while there was a howling draught. Most of these defects have been attended to, and an extensive amplifying system has partially improved the unsatisfactory nature of the acoustics; but the conversational style of debate does not flourish if one cannot hear what another speaker is saying except by bending the head towards a loud-speaker cunningly concealed in the carved woodwork on the back of the benches, and there have been occasions when microphones have been inadvertently left on, with the disconcerting result that remarks not intended for publication have echoed resoundingly through the Chamber. This remains a conspicuous defect of the new House of Commons, and it is extremely difficult to hear a Minister speaking from the Dispatch Box some thirty feet away when one is standing at the Bar of the House.

Behold, then, the House of Commons in session. The Speaker sits in his high Chair, no longer on altar steps, but still raised slightly above the benches. Before him sit the three Clerks at the Table which is placed between the two front benches. On his right sit the supporters of the Government, to his left the members of the Opposition. Facing him, several yards beyond the Table with its two Dispatch Boxes linked by a row of leather-bound books and the glittering Mace, there is the Bar of the House, on the left of which there sits the Serjeant at Arms. The Bar marks the limit of the House, although there are benches placed under the gallery facing the Chair, from which no Member may speak or interrupt. On both sides of the House, above the benches, there run two narrow galleries for the use of Members, officials and some members of the public. In front of the Speaker at the end of the House above the Bar, there are banked the galleries for Peers, Distinguished Strangers, and ordinary Strangers; behind and above him are the Press Galleries. And thus we have the Chamber of the House as it is to-day, a slightly larger and formalised version of St. Stephen's Chapel, but very much the child of that place where, by pure chance, the Commons received their first permanent home over four hundred years ago.

CHAPTER THREE

Honourable Members

"For every man who has taken part in the noble conflicts of parliamentary life, the chiefest ambition of all ambitions, whether in the majority or in the minority, must be to stand well with the House of Commons."

Sir William Harcourt, 1895

The House of Commons is composed of 630 men and women, each of whom represents approximately fifty thousand electors in constituencies in England, Scotland, Wales and Northern Ireland. No Parliament[1] can exist for more than five years, and in practice, very few last for more than four. The decision to dissolve Parliament and order the election of a new House of Commons rests in theory with the Queen, but in fact she is advised in this matter by the Prime Minister. The actual power to order a dissolution of Parliament is, therefore, in the hands of the Government, who can choose the moment which it thinks is best for its chances. If a Parliament should last for the full period of five years the Queen is obliged by law to end it, and order the election of another.

---

1 Parliament meets when the Queen—or her representatives—the Lords and the Commons are all present. "A Parliament" describes the period—never more than five years except in war—between elections. Each "Parliament" consists of one or more periods known as "Sessions", which normally last for a year, usually from the beginning of another, but it is popularly—and inaccurately—used to describe the Parliamentary holidays, properly called "adjournments", which take place at Christmas, Easter, Whitsun and the late Summer.

When the Queen "prorogues" Parliament, she orders it to cease holding meetings until a certain date; when she "dissolves" Parliament she ends its existence, and another one has to be elected in its place.

In the House of Commons the Member is a privileged person. He possesses, in common with all his fellow-Members, the actual Privileges of freedom of speech (in that he cannot be sued for libel or slander for anything he says in the House), freedom from arrest (which is of little importance to-day, since it does not extend to arrest or imprisonment for indictable offences), and exemption from serving on juries and attending as a witness in the Law Courts (this exemption is usually ignored). Of these Privileges, by far the most important is that of freedom of speech. The law of slander is very strict in this country, and the principle that no Member should be afraid of saying in the House what he thinks about an individual or group of individuals is a very important one. It is, however, a privilege that should not be abused or Parliament would be regarded with contempt, and the House as a whole is strongly critical of Members who do so.

The Member is saluted by the policemen on his way to the House, and has the traffic held back so that he can hasten to the Palace of Westminster; in the House itself he is referred to as "the Honourable Member," or the "Right Honourable Member" if he is a Privy Councillor, the "Honourable and Learned Member" if he is a barrister, or the "Honourable and Gallant Member" if he is a commissioned officer in any of the armed services. He is protected by the rules of the House from being called—at least, in so many words—a liar or a fool by a fellow-Member; his letters to Ministers are treated with consideration, and in his constituency he is regarded with a certain respect as "our Member," even by people who detest him and his politics. All this comes to an abrupt and unpleasant end when Parliament is dissolved and he has to present himself to his constituents for re-election.

The old Parliament is dissolved by Royal Proclamation, and the date for the meeting of the new one is named. On the same evening that the Proclamation is officially published in the *London Gazette*, the Queen's Writ is sent to every Peer and Bishop entitled to a summons to the House of Lords, as well as to every Returning Officer in each constituency. This official—usually the sheriff, mayor, or other local dignitary—is responsible for the proper conduct of the election in his constituency. He is called the Returning Officer because of his duty to write the name and address of the successful candidate on the back of the Queen's Writ and *return* it to the Clerk of the Crown at the Crown Office in Chancery. No Member may take his seat until this document has been received, for, although he may be famous, and his victory reported throughout the world, it is upon the written testimony of the Returning Officer alone that he is entitled to take his seat in the House of Commons.

In theory, almost anyone over the age of twenty-one can stand for Parliament, provided that he is not a (certified) lunatic, a convict, peer of the realm, judge, civil servant or clergyman of the Church of England, and can produce £150 as a deposit—which is returned to him if he gets over one-eighth of the votes cast—and the signatures of a proposer, seconder, and eight electors. But in effect no candidate outside the three main political parties—Labour, Conservative, and Liberal—stands much of a chance of even salvaging his deposit, let alone of winning a seat. Election expenses are rigidly controlled—in boroughs, to £450 and a further 1 ½d. per elector; in counties, to £450 and a further 2d. per elector; the candidate is allowed £100 for his personal expenses—but in the case of official party candidates much, if not all, of these are paid for by the party he represents, which also provides him with posters and other assistance, while the independent candidate would have to find much of this money himself. Expenses between elections, when he is "nursing" the constituency and making himself known in the district by making speeches, opening bazaars, and fulfilling other engagements, are entirely his responsibility, and then, of course, there is his £150 deposit, which the independent candidate stands an excellent chance of losing. It is not very surprising, in these circumstances, that independent candidates are now comparatively rare, and the abolition of the University Seats in 1948 has dealt the final blow to independency.

The election itself, although it may take only a few weeks, is the end of a long and involved proceeding which has probably lasted for several months. Virtually the only way for a man or woman to enter the House of Commons to-day is to affiliate himself or herself to one of the main political parties and then to find a local constituency organisation which will select him for their candidate.

Whenever their candidate dies or resigns, the local party association starts to look round for a replacement. The Central Office of the party in London sends a list of recommended candidates, but the association is perfectly free to ignore this if it so wishes. Circumstances vary in different parties and even in different constituencies, but the usual procedure is as follows. The local party agent—who is paid by party funds, and is responsible for the affairs of the party in his constituency—and the Chairman of the association plough through the list of possible candidates; if the seat is held by the party, the number of these hopefuls may be very great. They choose a few—usually about twenty or so, but often less—who seem the most likely. They submit the names to a Selection Committee which has been set up by the association, and this body cuts down the list even further, until only a handful remain. These are invited to appear before the Committee for a personal interview, which often takes the form of a brief speech. The Committee then choose their candidate, and present him to the full association for approval; this is usually a formality, but there have been occasions when ungrateful associations have expressed criticism of the Selection Committee's choice. Then, if the party's Central Office approve the choice, the victor of this curious hurdle-race is announced to the world as the party's "prospective candidate" for the constituency.

In the selection of their candidate—particularly if he is likely to be the next Member—the local association carries an immense responsibility, and it cannot be pretended that discharged satisfactorily and conscientiously. In some cases a democratic appearance has cloaked sheer pressure politics, and in some others the reasons which prompted the choice of the successful candidate were farcical. The late Lord Norwich (Duff Cooper) has described his excursion to the Conservatives of Stroud in 1924, and his depressing experience has been shared by many aspirants before and since.

. . . I had imagined having to answer some searching questions about Bills then before the House of Commons, with the details of which I should be ill-acquainted, and I had even equipped myself with a few facts about agriculture, a great subject about which I was woefully ignorant. I was therefore relieved when the small party who received me, some six or seven ladies and gentlemen, only enquired concerning my health, my religion, and the amount I was prepared to contribute to local expenses. When I say that they enquired concerning my religion I should make it plain that they wanted only to be assured that I was not a Roman Catholic. For the majority of English people there are only two religions, Roman Catholic, which is wrong, and the rest, which don't matter. I was able to give them the required assurances concerning health and religion and I undertook to contribute £300 a year to the local association, which I hoped I should be able to do out of my parliamentary salary. They were very polite, and as I travelled back to London I thought, with characteristic optimism, how well I should get to know that journey in the days to come. I did not have long to cherish the illusion, nor did I ever make the same journey again. Two days later I learnt that an older, possibly wiser and certainly much richer candidate had been selected . . .[1]

There have been determined and successful efforts by all political parties to improve the machinery by which candidates are chosen by local associations, but even after these improvements it cannot be denied that this is still a weak link in the democratic chain. The choice of many Members of Parliament lies in the hands of a very few people, and even if these were all possessed of outstanding public experience and were utterly unprejudiced—which they rarely are—half-an-hour is not enough time in which to judge if an individual is qualified to be a Member of Parliament.

Every General Election is dreaded by the average M.P. and longed for by every candidate. For the one it may be the end; for the

1 Duff Cooper: *Old Men Forget*, page 128.

other, the beginning. Both are now on level terms; both are "candidates," and entitled to be booed, jeered, heckled, and questioned by the merest hobbledehoy. On Nomination Day, when the official papers (including the £150) are handed in at the Town Hall, the candidates and their supporters meet, and hold a somewhat strained conversation. There then follow the weeks of knocking at doors, trudging pavements, beaming at children and photographers, speaking at little meetings in village halls or institutes. "The combination of anxiety and tedium is very trying," Duff Cooper has written. "The solitary topic of conversation, to which, however hard one may try to avoid it, one always returns, the good idea which suddenly strikes one's supporters, their hopes and fears and petty quarrels, the rumours of one's opponent's successes, the one thing that should have been done and has been forgotten, the great mistake that has been made that it is too late to rectify, the vast accumulation of daily annoyances culminating in the evening's speeches, which are followed by sleepless nights of pondering over possibly unwise utterances, all these build up an atmosphere of nightmare through which the distant polling day shines with promise of deliverance."[1]

On Polling Day—the name stems from the time when the heads (polls) of the electors were counted—there is a last hectic flurry of activity by the candidate's helpers. The polling stations are open early in the morning until nine o'clock in the evening, and although the vote is secret, the party "canvassers," who have been knocking at doors for weeks and distributing party documents, have a pretty good idea of who their supporters are, and if they have failed to vote by six o'clock or so they are knocked up again and urged to vote before the polling stations close. In most towns the counting of the votes starts almost as soon as they have been collected in the Town Hall in the black Ballot Boxes, and the result may be declared within an hour or so; in most counties, however, the boxes have to be collected from the scattered polling stations, and counting does not start until the following morning.

As the votes are counted, they are placed in separate piles beneath

---

1 *Old Men Forget*, page 135.

the names of the individual candidates. The Returning Officer and his assistants keep a careful check on the counting, and he acts as arbitrator in the case of any "spoilt" votes, or when it is difficult to decide for whom the vote has been cast. After the elections are over, the votes are kept for a year and a day in the Victoria Tower at the Palace of Westminster in case of disputes.

In Britain the electors may vote for only one candidate, and the single candidate with the most votes wins the election, even if those cast for the other candidates (if there are more than one) add up to many more. It is quite possible—and often happens—that a political party has a majority of seats in the House of Commons, but a minority of votes cast in the country. In 1950, for example, the Labour Party had a majority of eight in the Commons; in 1951 the party increased its total vote in the country, but the Conservatives had a majority in the Commons of sixteen over Labour and Liberal.[1]

After the last vote has been counted, the Returning Officer informs the candidates of the result, and asks if any of them want a recount; this is only requested in the case of a very close fight, and is a harrowing business for the candidates. The Returning Officer then announces the figures publicly, and the candidates make little speeches, in which they are meant by tradition to thank the Returning Officer and his assistants, congratulate the other candidates, and say something to their supporters. The Returning Officer then returns the Queen's Writ to the Clerk of the Crown, informing him that Mr. X of such-and-such an address has been elected to serve in the present Parliament for the Y Division.

The first few weeks of his membership are probably the most delightful a Member of Parliament experiences. Everyone is very kind and everything is new. The vast Palace of Westminster is opened to him. Old Members show him the Chamber and offices of the House, and introduce him to other Members, some of whom

---

1 In the 1950 General Election, 13,295,736 electors voted Labour, 12,501,983 voted Conservative, and 2,621,489 voted Liberal. There were 315 Labour M.P.s, 298 Conservative, and 9 Liberals, giving the Labour Government a majority of only 8 over both Opposition parties. In the 1951 Election, nearly fourteen million people voted Labour, and although slightly fewer voted Conservative, the Conservatives had a majority of 24 Members in the Commons over Labour. In the 1955 and 1959 Elections, however, the Conservatives had a majority both of the popular vote and of M.P.s.

he has hitherto admired at a distance, or whom he has just been castigating in the elections as the embodiment of perfidy. Every Member is anxious to inform his colleagues of the infamous accusations of his defeated opponents and his own unanswerable replies; there is a wonderful *bonhomie*, and the new Member is caught up in this infectious atmosphere. Already, perhaps, he is pondering his maiden speech.

> All the world looked kind,
> As it will look sometimes with the first stare,
> Which youth would not act ill to keep in mind.[1]

Members who enter the House after a by-election miss this wonderful, but, alas, all too brief, period.

The first duty of the new House of Commons is to elect its Speaker. On the afternoon of the day ordered by the Royal Proclamation which dissolved the old Parliament, the House meets with the Mace "below the Table." The Speaker's Chair is empty, and the three Clerks sit impassively behind the Table. At half past two the Head Doorkeeper advances to the Bar of the House, and shouts above the babel, "Black Rod." The Gentleman Usher of the Black Rod, to give him his full title, is an officer of the Royal Household who acts as an official of the House of Lords, and who has responsibilities similar to those of the Serjeant at Arms in the Commons.[2] He is the messenger of the Lords to the Commons when the presence of the Lower House is requested—or demanded, if the Sovereign is present—in the House of Lords. He carries a black ebony wand with a golden lion on the top as his staff of office, and as he approaches the Commons the door is slammed unceremoniously in his face and he knocks three times on it with his staff. "Who is there?" inquires the Serjeant at Arms, peering suspiciously through a grille in the door. "Black Rod," replies the Gentleman Usher, who is then permitted to enter the House. The tradition of locking Black Rod out is popularly supposed to be the

---

1 Byron: Don Juan.
2 See pages 59–62.

result of the invasion of the House by Charles I and his soldiers in 1642, since when the Commons have been suspicious of allowing Royal messengers to enter the House unless they are alone. What is certain is that the custom now represents the caution of the Commons when Royal messengers are concerned and its right to bar its doors against them.

Conversation dies down in the Chamber, and Members hear Black Rod's three imperious knocks on the door, and then, after a pause, while the doors are opened, see him advance up the Floor of the House, bowing to the empty Chair. He halts before the Table and informs Members that the presence "of this Honourable House"—bowing deeply to both sides—is requested in the House of Peers. The Clerk of the House rises and follows Black Rod out of the Chamber on his way back to the Lords, and Members form up behind him in a long line, walking two abreast across the Members' Lobby, down the short corridor to the Central Lobby, through the Lords' Lobby and into the House of Lords.

At the Bar "the faithful Commons" hear the Lord Chancellor read out the Royal instruction to them to proceed to the election of a Speaker, and then, again led by the Clerk, they return to their House to fulfil this duty.

The election of the Speaker in modern times has tended to become something of a formality. If the Government and the Opposition are unable to agree upon a candidate—assuming that the Speaker of the last Parliament is not seeking re-election—each party produces their own, and the debate and division follow normal party lines. In the case of two recent Speakers the Government and Opposition have been unable to agree, and although the Opposition did not put forward a rival candidate in 1959, they expressed criticism of the Government's action in proposing as Speaker a candidate who had held Ministerial rank, particularly in view of the fact that his predecessor—Mr. Speaker Morrison—had also been an ex-Minister.

The actual election of a new Speaker is, therefore, the culmination of a period of consultation between the political parties, and in these discussions the views of influential and experienced Members of the House are often sought. It is a tradition of the House that no Minister should propose a Speaker. When the younger Pitt, then Prime Minister, wished to propose Addington to the Chair in 1789, the Clerk opposed this suggestion, warning Addington that "an invidious use may be made to represent you as the friend of the Minister rather than the choice of the House."

The Clerk of the House opens the proceedings of the election of the Speaker by rising and pointing dumbly to a back-bench Member who, addressing the Clerk, moves that "Mr.——do take the Chair of this House as Speaker;" when he has finished, the Clerk stabs his finger at another Member, who seconds the Motion. If there is another candidate, the procedure is repeated, and both the Prime Minister and Leader of the Opposition may make brief speeches. After the candidates have addressed the House, the Clerk breaks his silence to put the Question "That Mr.——do take the Chair of this House as Speaker", and orders a division if necessary. (If there is only one candidate, no Question is put by the Clerk.)

The proposer and seconder of the successful candidate then seize him and lead him to the Chair: in accordance with tradition, the victim puts up a token struggle before he is deposited on the lower step of the Chair. Before taking the Chair he expresses his gratitude for the great honour the House has done him, and then receives the congratulations of the party leaders before adjourning the House.

He is now Mr. Speaker-elect, for he has not received the Royal approval, and on the day following his election he wears Court dress and a small bob-wig, similar to those worn by barristers. Again the Commons are summoned to the Bar of the House of Lords, when Mr. Speaker-elect informs the Lord Chancellor that the Commons "in the exercise of their undoubted right and privilege" have proceeded to the choice of a Speaker and have chosen himself, "and I therefore present myself at your Lordships' Bar, humbly submitting myself for Her Majesty's gracious approbation." The Lord Chancellor replies that "Her Majesty is so fully sensible of your zeal for the public service, and your undoubted efficiency to execute all the arduous duties of the position to which the faithful Commons have selected you to discharge, that she does most readily approve and confirm your election as Speaker." Mr. Speaker then asks for the ancient privileges of the Commons—freedom of speech, freedom from arrest, and freedom for their Speaker to have personal access to the Queen—which are duly granted. The procession then returns to the Commons, with the Mace, which up to now has been held by the Serjeant at Arms in the crook of his arm, carried high on his shoulder. In the House Mr. Speaker disappears for a moment behind the Chair, and then reappears in his full regalia, with black gown and full-bottomed wig and takes the Chair amid cheers while the Mace is placed on the Table. Mr. Speaker then informs the House of the proceedings "in another place" as the House of Lords is called in the Commons, and then takes the Oath of Allegiance to the Queen. He then signs the roll—a long roll of parchment folded into a book—and is followed by the members of the Government, the Opposition front bench, and back-benchers. Each Member takes the Oath or affirms, signs the roll, and shakes hands with Mr. Speaker. Until this ritual is completed—it usually takes at least two days—no Member is entitled to take any part in the proceedings of the House, and if he does so, he is liable to a savage fine and to vacate his seat "as though he were dead."

After the intriguing procedure of the election of the Speaker the new Member sees the splendid pageantry of the State Opening of Parliament, when the Queen reads the Queen's Speech—which is written by the Government, and which contains its programme for the forthcoming Session—to both Houses assembled in the House of Lords. The Commons then debate the speech for several days, but not until they have formally read the Outlawries Bill a first time. This obscure Bill "for the more effectual preventing Clandestine Outlawries" is never heard of again, and although its origin is veiled in some mystery, it is regarded as a symbol of the right of the Commons to proceed to business before they discuss the Queen's Speech.

The Parliamentary glitter fades all too quickly for the backbench

Member. He discovers that the accommodation provided for him is not over-generous. There is a large but usually overcrowded Library, dining, smoking, and chess rooms and cafeteria, and, as the Palace of Westminster is a Royal Palace, the ordinary licensing laws which limit the sale of drink to certain hours do not apply to Members and officers of the House. There are interview rooms which Members may book, and each Member has a small locker for his papers and a hook for his overcoat. These are the limits of the accommodation provided for him. He has no private room—unless he is a Minister or a Chairman of an important Committee—and not even a telephone. If a constituent, his wife, or a friend want to get hold of him he is sought by one of the Badge Messengers, so-called because they wear a gold badge of office across the white shirts of the evening dress which they wear on duty. He collects his post from the Post Office just off the Members' Lobby, and may have to dictate to his secretary in one of the corridors or lobbies. If he does not live in London he will have to find accommodation reasonably near to Westminster, and if he is not particularly well-off this can be a trying and difficult business. His parliamentary salary is £1750 a year, of which £750 is allowed tax-free for expenses, and he has free travel allowances for journeys between Westminster and his constituency. This salary cannot be called generous, and indeed it can barely cover expenses if the Member is conscientious. A considerable number of Members—lawyers and journalists in particular—can continue their professions almost without interruption, but there are many who cannot do this, and who find that they are far worse off financially than they were before they were elected. These discoveries, and the sheer inconvenience of constantly travelling between his constituency and London, tend to damp the exhilaration of the new Member.

There are other, less obvious, factors which help the process of disillusionment. The atmosphere of the Palace itself is somewhat chilling, and the anonymity of the average Member once the first excitement has worn off can lead to frustration. He finds that hardly anyone knows who he is and even fewer care; his majority is better known than his name, and the Whips are more interested in his vote than in his voice. He finds that the House is settling down to a humdrum existence in which he plays little, if any, part. He is baffled by the Procedure, sits long conscientious hours in the Chamber, tramps through the division lobbies, sits disconsolately in interminable Standing Committees, and answers floods of constituency correspondence. This boredom is far greater for a supporter of the Government than for a member of the Opposition. "Even in a period of political activity there is small scope for the supporters of a Government," Sir Winston Churchill has written.[1] "The Whips do not want speeches, but votes. The Ministers regard an oration in their praise or defence as only one degree less tiresome than an attack. The earnest party man becomes a silent drudge, tramping at intervals through lobbies to record his vote and wondering why he came to Westminster at all. Ambitious youth diverges into criticism and even hostility, or seeks an outlet for its energies elsewhere." This may not be the experience of all M.P.s, but it is certainly that of a great number. It is the feeling that the individual Member has hardly any direct influence which really hurts; a Civil Servant, a councillor in a local authority, a town clerk, all seem to have more actual influence. Some Members become so depressed with this apparent state of affairs that they spend too much time in their constituencies and too little at Westminster, while others try to gain a certain notoriety by causing trouble, putting down Motions and Questions with sullen enthusiasm.

The ability of the House of Commons to deflate the self-importance of the individual Member is almost calculated, and in this respect it has an extraordinary resemblance to a school. New boys should be seen and not heard, and until they are accepted on their own merits they should behave with modesty. When Mr. Nigel Nicolson was standing at the Bar of the House in 1952, waiting to take his seat after a by-election, a senior Member whispered to him, "In a few minutes you will walk behind the Speaker's Chair into the obscurity from which you should probably never have emerged."

---

1 *Lord Randolph Churchill* (one volume edition, 1951), page 66.

It was my first lesson in parliamentary deflation. To come from the concentrated arc-lights, the excitement, the triumph, of an election, to the goal of your ambition, and find that the size of your majority is better known than your name, is an immediate reminder that you are of so little significance that when you die or lose your seat, you will probably be replaced as easily as a broken window-pane ... it is not only the antiquity of Parliament which cuts a man down in size. It is its terrible power to sum up character and detect fraud.[1]

The problem of the maiden speech—the first speech which the Member makes in the House—is a terrible one for the sensitive man or woman. Some friends advise him to "get it over quickly;" others urge him to bide his time; he must not speak too quietly, nor should he shout; he must not be provocative or controversial, but his speech should not be colourless, and so on. And then there are the awful precedents of maiden speeches which have ended in disaster. Cobbett made his "maiden" on his first night in the House, and, having listened to a debate in which all the House of Commons swells had taken part, opened up with the words, "Mr. Speaker, it appears to me that since I have been sitting here I have heard a great deal of vain and unprofitable conversation!" Then there was Sir Richard Temple, who, after a distinguished career in India, entered the House in 1886, and noted in his diary that "In the Commons I wish to comport myself modestly and quietly." He then made his maiden speech on the first night of the opening Session of a new Parliament! The House does not easily forgive presumption of this kind, and although Cobbett recovered from his hideous lapse, Temple did not.

The temptation to "get it over" is very great. Disraeli called the Commons "the most chilling and nerve-destroying audience in the world," and the great Macaulay wrote that "there is not a more terrible audience in the world." "The great speakers fill me with despair," Edward Gibbon, the historian, wrote, "the bad ones with terror." As a result, he never made a speech, although a Member

---

1 Nigel Nicolson: *People and Parliament*, page 62.

for eight years. Lord North's son was one of many Members who started well enough, then lost the trend of his argument, and completely "dried up;" "I lost my recollection," he later explained, "and could see nothing but the Speaker's wig, which swelled and swelled and swelled until it covered the whole House. I then sank back on my seat and never attempted another speech." Another Member said that when he saw the Speaker's wig surrounded by blue flames he knew it was time to sit down.

In the House every Member except those on the front benches who can use the Dispatch Box to put their papers on, speaks from his place, addressing Mr. Speaker or the Chairman. His audience is not in front of him, as at a public meeting, but all around him. There is usually a continuous movement in the Chamber. Members are constantly going in and out, others are talking to each other; some are seeking the advice of the Clerks on procedural matters; the doorkeepers are constantly moving around with their sheafs of messages, which they pass down the benches. The orator faces his opponents, and although one or two of his colleagues on his benches may turn round encouragingly, this is usually more disconcerting than helpful. As Sir Alan Herbert has remarked, "It is like making a speech in a beehive."[1]

A maiden speaker who is overcome by nervousness is always treated with sympathy by the House, who knows what he is going through, but the Member who tries to harangue it in a "maiden," or to introduce controversial party political matter, is more roughly treated. Disraeli shared with Steele—a famous journalist of the beginning of the eighteenth century—the doubtful distinction of having his "maiden" howled down, and, crying, "The time will come when you *shall* hear me!" was obliged to resume his seat. This was perhaps just, for Disraeli had recently described a maiden effort of one of his colleagues, a Mr. Gibson Craig, in pitiless terms for the amusement of his family. The unfortunate Craig "rose, stared like a stuck pig and said nothing. His friends cheered; he stammered; all cheered; then there was a dead and awful pause, and then he sat down, and that was his performance." In 1906 a

---

1 Sir Alan Herbert: *Independent Member*, page 47.

Liberal Member who seconded the Motion for the Humble Address, by tradition always an uncontroversial speech, made a violent attack upon the Conservative Opposition, and was excitedly cheered by the mass of new Liberal Members. It was a gross breach of Parliamentary etiquette for a maiden speaker thus to address the House, and the Conservatives sat in an angry silence. When Mr. Joseph Chamberlain rose to open the debate from the Opposition Front Bench he warmly praised the speech of the proposer of the motion, which, he said, had set a precedent for such speeches. "The Hon. Member who seconded the Motion," he went on quietly, choosing his words with a cold deliberation, "also created a precedent, which I trust will never again be followed in this House." The offender only made one more speech in the House, which was listened to in contemptuous silence, and disappeared, unmourned and unnoticed, at the next election. The Commons can be savagely cruel to those who try to ride roughshod over their unwritten traditions, and only an F. E. Smith can turn his maiden speech into a blazing denunciation of his political opponents and get away with it. Smith's maiden speech, made in 1906, is a Parliamentary legend. He filled the House, routed the Government benches, whipped up his Conservative colleagues to an intense excitement, and when he sat down his Parliamentary reputation was made. Since "Single-Speech" Hamilton of the eighteenth century, who had a similar triumph but never made another speech in the Commons, no maiden speaker has so gripped the House. But the risks of failure are so tremendous, that it takes a man of either exceptional courage or exceptional stupidity to make such a speech, and Smith told his wife beforehand that if it was a failure he would have to remain silent for at least three years to let the House forgive him for his crime.

When the new Member has assimilated the advice so generously bestowed upon him by his colleagues, he "works up" a subject, and devotes great care to it. Before The Day he writes to the Speaker, asking to be "called" in the debate, and he spends an agonising morning. After a tasteless lunch he goes to the House early to make sure of his seat by attending Prayers. Other Members notice his pale face and bundle of notes, and some pass reassuring messages along the benches. After Question Time and any statements are over the debate begins, and the maiden speaker has to endure the exquisite agony of hearing all his arguments brought out by the Government and Opposition spokesmen who open the debate in turn from the respective Dispatch Boxes. Maiden speakers are usually called early in the debate to lessen the misery of waiting, and as soon as the second front-bencher has sat down to the accompaniment of "'ear, 'ears" from his supporters, a dozen Members leap to their feet and gaze stonily at the Chair; the Speaker calls "Mr. Z"—one of the very few occasions when Members are referred to by name in the House—the other Members sit down, and the "maiden" is on. "When the appointed day came, and the appointed hour," Lord Samuel has recorded, "and I rose from my place on one of the back benches on the Opposition side, the Speaker, the Members and all my surroundings completely vanished from view. Automatically my prepared opening sentences uttered themselves. After a moment or two someone out of the mist kindly said, "Hear, hear;" that recalled me to myself, and I went on more conscious of what I was saying."[1] At length the ordeal is over, the speaker sinks back into his place, limp and exhausted, while other Members jump up and stare at the Speaker, who calls one of them. It is a very strong tradition of the House that maiden speeches are warmly praised, and although there are occasions when the following speaker has to struggle with his conscience, tradition usually triumphs. When Mr. Herbert Morrison (now Lord Morrison of Lambeth) made a fierce maiden speech, the Member who was called immediately after him remarked coldly that "It is the custom of this House to congratulate a maiden speaker. Sir, I do so."

But we will assume that our Member's "maiden" is a success, and he sits down to what the newspapers call "loud cheers," but which actually are "'ear, 'ears," sounding to the visitors in the Galleries more like "ya, ya." Messages of congratulation are passed along the benches, and a wonderful feeling of elation steals over

---

1 Lord Samuel: *Memoirs*, page 42.

the Member. After a few minutes a long buff envelope is passed to him; it is a message from the Official Reporter, asking him to come up to his office as there were one or two passages in his speech which were difficult to follow in the Gallery. The Member waits until the speech of the man who followed him is over, and then, bowing to the Chair and clutching the envelope, leaves the House and goes to the Official Reporter's room above the Chamber, where he is presented with pages of typescript on duck-egg-blue paper. This is his speech, and he goes over it with the shorthand writers who took it down, correcting any mistakes which they may have made. The checking of a speech in cold blood is not a pleasant task, for even the most splendid phrase can look rather ridiculous in print. The Member is now entitled to take an active part in the work of the House, for he has crossed the first, and in some ways the highest, hurdle in his House of Commons career.

"You have come to the dullest place on earth," Lord Randolph Churchill said at the height of his fame to a new Member; "but there are compensations." Its "dullness" stems from the fact that it is, for nine-tenths of the time, a place of business, where there are no dramatic "scenes" and no impassioned speeches, but just hard, meticulous, unspectacular work in which proposals of the Government are carefully examined and discussed. The "compensations" are many for the man who comes to love the House of Commons; for the man who does not and cannot, there is nothing. The House has an uncanny ability of finding out which Members admire it and are proud to belong to it, and those who detest it; no amount of smooth words can disguise this fatal defect. It is impossible to love the House of Commons all the time; indeed there are always occasions when its greatest admirers actively loathe it, and vow they will never stand any more of its rudeness, pettiness and stupidity, but within a short time the magic of the place reasserts itself. The man who really loves the House of Commons could employ the famous line of Addison to describe his feeling; "There is no living with thee, nor without thee."

Success in the House comes only to a comparatively few of its

Members. An individual Member may from time to time succeed in capturing "the ear of the House" and savour for a short time that incomparable sensation. But a persistent hold upon the attention and respect of the House over a number of years calls for an exceptional combination of qualities. It is not possible to catalogue these, although sincerity, ability, courage and humour are of high importance, for, as Lord Rosebery wrote of the elder Pitt, "It is not merely the thing that is said, but the man who says it that counts, the character which breathes through the sentences." Horace Walpole was present in the House in 1755 when Pitt made one of his greatest speeches, and recorded that "His eloquence like a torrent long obstructed burst forth with more commanding impetuosity . . . There was more humour, wit, vivacity, fine language, more boldness—in short, more astonishing perfections than even you who are used to him can conceive." The Parliamentary skill of Sir Robert Peel, on the other hand, who occupied a dominant position in the House in the 1830's and early 1840's, lay in his ability to adapt himself to the changing moods of the House. "This remarkable man," his great opponent, Disraeli, has recorded, "who in private life was constrained, and often awkward, who could never address a public meeting or make an after-dinner speech without being ill at ease, and generally saying something stilted, or even a little ridiculous, in the senate was the readiest, easiest, most flexible and adroit of men. He played upon the House of Commons, as on an old fiddle."[1] This ability to change the course of a prepared speech to fit in with the mood of the House is far more difficult than anyone who has not been intimately connected with the House can appreciate. There have been some great Parliamentary figures like the elder Pitt and Sir Winston Churchill who have imposed their own mood upon that of the House, and whose speeches were meticulously prepared beforehand. Men of this stature have to use their experience of the House to anticipate its mood, and if they miscalculate it—as both Pitt and Churchill did on occasion—the result is a Parliamentary disaster.

"Oratory" has fallen upon bad times, and men seem to gain

---

1 *Lord George Bentinck*, page 48.

pleasure in saying, "I am no orator as Brutus was." Really great oratory, of the Pitt, John Bright, Gladstone, Churchill type has almost vanished, yet the House of Commons will always be enthralled by the real thing. In the Crimean War in the 1850's Bright made one of the most magnificent speeches in Parliamentary history in opposition to the war. "The Angel of Death has been abroad throughout the land," he said to a hushed House of Commons; "you may almost hear the beating of his wings." Afterwards, when being congratulated, he said, "Ah, yes; but if I had said 'the flapping of his wings' they would have laughed." The margin between triumph and catastrophe is always very narrow in House of Commons oratory.

Whenever one attempts to answer the question, why did so-and-so succeed in the House while another man failed, one is inevitably brought back to Rosebery's remark about "the character which breathes through the sentences." The elder Pitt secured such a mastery over the House that when he once started a great speech with the words, "Sugar, Mr. Speaker," and there was some tittering, he repeated the word "sugar" three times, and then, turning a freezing eye on the silenced titterers, asked, "Who *now* presumes to laugh at sugar?" Cardinal Newman, a great divine of the last century, once wrote of the perfect author that:

> He always has the right word for the right idea, and never a word too much. If he is brief, it is because few words suffice; if he is lavish of them, still each word has its mark, and aids, not embarrasses, the vigorous march of his elocution. He expresses what all feel, but all cannot say, and his sayings pass into proverbs among his people, and his phrases become household words and idioms of their daily speech,

and this doctrine of perfection should be applied to Parliamentary oratory.

The friendliness of the small world of the House of Commons is one of its most warming features. Assuming that the Member is reasonably modest, trustworthy and unbigoted, he will find friends easily on both sides of the House. The intimacy of the Chamber itself, and the corridors and lobbies which surround it, make for easy contact and friendliness, which would be endangered if each Member had his own office and telephone. The new Member will find that the building fairly hums with gossip, much of which has no relation whatever to politics; he is warned about the bores who grapple one with hoops of iron in the Bar, Smoking Room or Lobby; he will discover that it is not always safe to speak freely to some journalists or even a certain Lobby Correspondent,[1] whose charm of manner disguises an untrustworthy character. He will learn to "translate" the printed "Whip" which he receives each week, so that he need not waste his time hanging around the Palace waiting for a division which will never take place; he discovers the art of "pairing," the unofficial system by which Members of each party arrange not to vote within certain times so that they can get away from the Palace. Above all, he learns that presumption and insincerity are the greatest of House of Commons sins.

Reference has been made to the Whips, and this should be explained. The title comes from the phrase of the hunting field, to describe the man—"the whipper-in"—whose job it is to look after the hounds and keep them *together* in the field. The two major political parties each have about twelve Members who are appointed to the Whips' Office. In the Conservative Party they are appointed by the Leader of the Party: in the Labour Party, the Chief Whip is elected by Labour M.P.s, and he appoints his assistants. Most of the Government Whips have Government posts. The Chief Whip—usually called the Patronage Secretary—is the Parliamentary Secretary to the Treasury, five of his assistants are Lords Commissioners of the Treasury, and three more hold positions in the Royal Household as Treasurer, Controller, and Vice-Chamberlain. Another three or four are unpaid assistant Whips: all the Opposition Whips are unpaid.

---

1 A select band of newspapermen who are allowed to enter the Members' Lobby. Their job is not to report debates but to gather information from Members. There are about twenty of these correspondents, and they are usually on very close terms with individual Members. They have a very high reputation for integrity, but there have been a few occasions when individual Lobby Correspondents have betrayed the trust placed in them.

The position of the Government Chief Whip is extremely important, as he is responsible for preparing the Government "time-table" as well as for ensuring that the Government can always obtain an adequate majority in the House. He is also the channel of communication with the Opposition, and these are known as "the usual channels." The Opposition may say, "We want a Vote of Censure on the Foreign Secretary;" the Chief Opposition Whip informs the Patronage Secretary, who says, "Will Tuesday do?" If the Opposition agree, the fact is announced in the House. Negotiations through "the usual channels" are almost continuous, and it is important that a good relationship should exist between the respective Chief Whips if the business of the House is to be arranged satisfactorily. The Government Chief Whip has the assistance of a small staff of civil servants from the Treasury who work closely with the Clerks, and who do not change when the Government does.

In the Whips' Office, each Whip has a special responsibility towards approximately thirty Members: these groups are usually divided geographically, and in the Labour Party the Whip for a particular group must be a Member for the area he "controls," but this rule does not apply with the Conservatives. There are a number of "Whips' runners" who are messengers employed to carry urgent messages and distribute party documents to Members: they also keep a check on the Members who are in the building by keeping a "roll" in the Members' Lobby; while the House is sitting there is always one Government Whip sitting by the door which leads out of the Lobby down to New Palace Yard to make sure that Members do not slip out and endanger the majority of the Government or the "quorum"—forty Members—of the House. If a Member calls attention to the fact that there are not forty Members in the Chamber, and forty do not assemble within four minutes—the division bells are rung and the policemen and messengers call "Count!"—the House is adjourned; if this occurs when Government business is being discussed the Government looks an ass and loses a valuable sitting day.

The duty of the Whips is not confined to keeping the party

Members hanging around the House. They communicate any information they may have gathered from back-benchers to the party leaders, and when trouble is brewing this is extremely important. They also pass on hints from the top to the rank and file, and so act as intermediaries between the leaders and the back-benchers. If a Member or group of Members are discontented, it is the duty of the Whips to warn the leaders of the party and try to soothe the worries of the displeased Members. When a Member votes against his party, the Chief Whip will look into the matter, and can summon the offender to a personal interview. The best Whips rule by persuasion rather than by intimidation, but they can make life quite unpleasant for a Member who persistently ignores their advice.

Every week each Member receives his party "Whip." This is a document which gives the details of the business for next week and also those of party meetings in the House. The printed "Whip" could take the following form:

Monday, 21st April	The House will meet at 2.30 p.m. Second Reading of the Merchant Shipping Bill.

There will be an important division at ten o'clock, and your attendance is particularly requested.

Tuesday, 22nd April.	The House will meet at 2.30 p.m. Debate on Foreign Affairs on the motion for the Adjournment of the House.

Your attendance is requested.

Wednesday, 23rd April.	The House will meet at 2.30 p.m. Conclusion of the Debate on Foreign Affairs.

There will be a most important division or divisions at ten o'clock, and your attendance throughout the Sitting is particularly requested.

	Consideration of the Agriculture (Threshers and Balers) Order, 196—.

Your attendance throughout the debate until 11.30 is requested.

From this document the Member will realise that there will be a division on Monday which he must attend unless he can get the Whips of both parties to agree to a "pair." It is a "two-line whip," and he must have a good reason for not being present to vote. On Tuesday, the opening day of a two-day debate on Foreign Affairs, no vote is expected, but he should be present unless he obtains the leave of the Whips to go. On the Wednesday, there is a "three-line whip," and this division he must not fail to attend; if he does not vote, then the Whips will take a very grave view of his failure unless he has a first-class excuse.

A good Whip has to know his charges well. One man may need careful handling, as he has a reputation for easily taking offence, another is rather lazy, and must be talked to with firmness; a third may be suspicious of the Whips and needs to be treated gently; a fourth may be a completely selfish career politician who enjoys a reputation for independence, and who should probably be left alone until he commits an act of flagrant disloyalty to the party, when he may have to be severely warned by the Whip. Disraeli used to be given a list of his supporters who were getting restive by his Whips, and he would make a point of having a word with them in the division lobby, using his famous charm to soothe their wounded feelings. Leaders of parties cannot be expected to follow the fortunes of all their supporters, and a Whip can cause great happiness if he surreptitiously warns a leading member of the party that X made a good speech last week, or Y has just published a book which got good reviews, and so on, so that the leader can either write a letter to the Member, or, even better, congratulate him personally. These touches all help to keep a political party running smoothly, and even the smallest details of management should not escape the attention of a good Whip.

The happiest time of the day at the House is often after the ten o'clock division. Members are excited and exhilarated by the debate, and congregate in the Members' Lobby, where the roar of conversation can be heard in the Central Lobby. The man who spoke well is slapped on the back and congratulated; friends come down from the galleries and are taken off for celebratory drinks.

Members chat in the Lobby, or form in little knots in the corridors, or fight the old Parliamentary battles in the Smoking Room. At length the cry of "Who Goes Home?" echoes down the corridors, and Members slowly disperse and leave the darkened Palace. It is at moments like this, when he feels that he is at the centre of events and part of the central fabric of Government, that the new Member realises the truth of the wonderful *camaraderie* of the House of Commons.

CHAPTER FOUR

Mr. Speaker, the Learned Clerks, and Officials

"Go, and assemble yourself together, and elect one, a discreet, wise and learned man, to be your Speaker."

Instruction to the Commons by the Lord Chancellor in the reign of Queen Elizabeth I.

Mr. Speaker is the most eminent of all Members of Parliament. Elected by his fellow-Members to serve as Speaker for the duration of a Parliament, he has a fine house in the Palace of Westminster, a salary of £5,750 a year, and the prospect of a pension and elevation to the House of Lords when he retires. Members, officials, and Strangers bow to him as he passes down the corridors of the Palace, and in the House he is listened to with respect. He is called the Speaker because he is the mouthpiece of the Commons. "May it please Your Majesty," Mr. Speaker Lenthall addressed King Charles I—the last reigning monarch who entered the Chamber—in 1642 when the King appeared in the House, "I have neither eyes to see nor tongue to speak in this place, but as the House is pleased to direct me, whose servant I am here." This declaration marked the change which had taken place in the position of the Speaker: from being the servant of the Crown he had become that of the House of Commons.

In the Chair, the Speaker is responsible for controlling the debates of the House, selecting Members to speak, ruling on points of order, proposing and putting the Question on all motions, and ordering divisions when his opinion that the Ayes or the Noes "have it" is challenged. Above all, he is the custodian of the rules of procedure which govern the conduct of the business of the House, and which are laid down by Standing Order or precedent. "The forms of proceeding," Mr. Speaker Onslow, the first of the great modern Speakers (1727–61), once remarked, "as instituted by our ancestors, operated as a check and control on the action of Ministers, and they were in many instances a shelter and a protection to the minority against the attempts of power."

The complete impartiality of the Speaker, although comparatively modern, is the most distinctive feature of the Chair. "I know how necessary it is for any man who aspires to fill that great office to lay aside all that is personal, all that is of party, all that savours of political predilection, and to subordinate everything to the great interests of the House at large, to maintain not only the written law, but that unwritten law which should appeal to, as it always does appeal to, the minds and consciences of the gentlemen of the House of Commons." This declaration by Mr. Speaker Peel upon entering his great Speakership (from 1884 to 1895) summarises the modern concept of the office. "I loved independency, and pursued it," Onslow once robustly declared. Since the time of Shaw-Lefevre (Speaker from 1839 to 1857) the impartiality of the Chair has been its most cherished and effective feature, and although Shaw-Lefevre once spoke in Committee on behalf of the Trustees of the British Museum—of which he was one—in 1856, and Mr. Speaker Denison actually voted in a division in 1870 against the Government, since those occasions the Speaker has kept aloof from even the least controversial of discussions.

As a general rule the Speaker is assisted to maintain his independence by being allowed an uncontested election in his constituency. Mr. Speaker Peel (a Liberal) was opposed by the Conservatives at Warwick and Leamington in 1885 on the somewhat dubious ground that as the constituency was a new one—there had just been a Redistribution Act which had altered many constituencies—it was desirable to test the political opinions of the new electors. He won a narrow victory by 372 votes, but refused to indulge in any political activity in the election. In 1895 another Liberal, Mr. Speaker Gully, was opposed at Carlisle by the Conservatives, his opponents claiming that their action was justified as, in their view, he had been forced on to the House by the Liberal Government and that in any event it was the responsibility of his party to find him a safe seat, his majority being a meagre 143. Mr. Asquith—later Prime Minister—described the action of the Conservatives as "a departure from the finer and better traditions of English public life," and Mr. Gully appealed to the sense of justice of the electors of Carlisle as he could not undertake a political campaign. To the general surprise, in an election in which the Conservatives triumphed almost everywhere, Gully actually increased his majority to 314. In 1935 Mr. Speaker Fitzroy, and in 1945, Mr. Speaker Clifton Brown, were opposed by official Labour candidates, but with these exceptions, the Speaker— although sometimes denied an unopposed election—has not been challenged by an official party candidate since 1895.

The Speaker, of course, remains a Member of Parliament, and it has sometimes been said that his constituents are "disfranchised," as their Member cannot air their grievances in the House, ask questions from Ministers, or indulge in any political activity. The answer to this charge is that no Member of Parliament is in a more favourable position to champion the interests of his constituents than Mr. Speaker, since a letter from him will receive more urgent treatment by a Government Department than that accorded to the average private Member. Furthermore, it is always possible for another Member to raise a matter on his behalf in the House, but this is rarely necessary. When Mr. Speaker Lowther confronted his constituents at Penrith in 1906 he said, "The Speaker, as you know, has no politics, and I forbear therefore from entering upon a discussion of any of the current topics of political controversy, but I hope and believe that in my hands your interests will be safe, and I can promise that my best endeavours will be put forth to serve you."

A Speaker who presents himself to the House at the beginning of a new Parliament for re-election is now by custom automatically chosen, even if the party which elected him has been defeated at the polls. Sir Robert Peel stated this doctrine in 1841, and it has not been altered since then. "I do not think it necessary," he told the House, "that the person elected to the Chair who had conscientiously and ably performed his duties should be displaced because his political opinions are not consonant to those of the majority of the House." Mr. A. J. Balfour threatened to destroy this tradition in 1895 in the case of the unfortunate Mr. Gully, but the threat was not carried out when the Conservatives returned with a majority. It is by the preservation of these unwritten traditions that the House has helped to preserve the unique authority of the Chair.

But the authority which the Speaker exercises is, in the last analysis, one of personality alone. He is given immense powers by the House. He can order a Member to resume his seat, leave the Chamber, and, in the event of persistent refusal to obey his commands, he can "name" the offender to the House. This power stems from a resolution of the House in 1693 to the effect that "in cases of such noise or disturbance, that Mr. Speaker do call upon the Member by name, making such disturbance, and that every such person shall incur the displeasure and censure of the House." In 1880 it was made a Standing Order, and the procedure is that if a Member disobeys the repeated warnings of the Chair, the Speaker says, "I name Mr. X for disregarding the authority of the Chair," and at once the Leader of the House—or the most senior Minister on the Treasury Bench—moves that the offender "be suspended from the service of this House." No debate is permitted; the Question is put forthwith on the motion which, if carried, means that the Member must not enter the precincts of the House for five sitting days.[1] In cases of really serious disorder— such as that which once occurred in the debates on the Suez Crisis of November 1956—the Speaker can suspend the sitting, or even adjourn the House until the next day.

A Speaker who makes excessive use of the powers of the Chair

---

1 Since 1926, the period has been five sitting days for the first offence, twenty for the second, and the remainder of the session on any subsequent occasion.

rarely improves his authority, and usually earns the dislike of the House. A weak Speaker, on the other hand, hoping to secure peace by conceding to pressure, falls into the opposite trap. A modern Speaker, when baffled by a point of order, replied that, "I must consult the Table" (in other words, the Clerks), and the House took strong exception to this evidence of weakness; whenever a point of order was subsequently raised by a Member there were mutterings of "consult the Table." Mr. Speaker Gully never recovered his authority after he had ordered the police to remove some Irish Members who had been suspended by the House and who had refused to leave the Chamber; the closing years of his term of office were marked by cries of "send for the police" whenever trouble arose.

There are few qualities common to the great Speakers except force of personality. Disraeli once said of Shaw-Lefevre that even "the rustle of his robes" was sufficient to quell an unruly Member. Peel ruled by intimidation; Brand (1872–84) by aloofness; and Lowther (1905–21) by firmness tempered with an excellent wit. Peel was undoubtedly the most awe-inspiring of modern Speakers. He had the physical advantage of height, a rich voice, piercing eyes and daunting red beard, and the House was almost frightened of him. When he was ordered to deliver a rebuke to the directors of a railway company who had infringed the Privileges of the House in 1892, he did so with such terrifying majesty that the offenders at the Bar were ashen-faced when he had finished. On another occasion, a shallow and self-seeking Member published a vitriolic attack upon Peel in a newspaper and was demolished in the House when Peel ordered him to stand in his place, recited his crimes, and, with quivering finger stabbing at the sullen recipient of his fury, ended, "And now, *forsooth*, under the guise of fulfilling a public duty, he charges me with the grossest offence possible for a man in my position." But a mere recital of incidents cannot adequately describe the extraordinary power that Peel wielded. The most remarkable tribute to it was paid in 1893 when fighting actually broke out in the Chamber when the House was in Committee. Peel was sent for, and, calmly entering the House, his presence at once stilled the uproar. Members expected a blistering rebuke for their conduct, delivered in the Speaker's most terrifying manner. Instead, he gently asked for information, accepted the apologies proffered by Members, and declared the incident closed.

Speaker Lowther achieved his authority by charm of manner, wit, and resolution. He once privately remarked that if the Speaker made a mistake in the House he should stand by his decision at the time, but, if necessary, apologise *the next day*. The subtlety of this tactic is well suited to the House, which rather likes a firm Speaker, but detests obstinacy. Few Speakers have had to occupy the Chair in a period of such political bitterness, but Lowther's authority rarely wavered.

It is the fickleness of the House of Commons, when allied to its complicated procedure, which makes the task of the Speaker so difficult. As a very experienced journalist has written, "There is nothing more surprising in the House of Commons than the uncertainty of its moods. There is no barometer to herald the approach of a Parliamentary storm. All of a sudden a hurricane bursts upon the House out of what seemed to be just a moment before the most tranquil of situations. It is these sudden emergencies—the sharp contact of strong character and untoward circumstances—that show the stuff of which the Speaker is really made; these sudden emergencies when human passions are fiercely aroused, and with him, and him alone, lies the task of subduing them."[1] Between these moments of crisis stretch hours of sheer tedium when a succession of impossibly dreary orators speechify to deserted benches. Sir Fletcher Norton (Speaker from 1770–80) used to groan aloud, "I am tired! I am weary! I am heartily sick of all this!" His cry has been echoed more or less silently by his predecessors and successors. Mr. Speaker Lowther used to mutter audibly when bored, and Mr. Speaker Fitzroy drummed his fingers noisily on the side of the Chair and glared darkly at the object of his wrath. But there is a type of House of Commons speaker who is utterly impervious to hints of these kind.

The Speaker is assisted in his formidable and delicate task by

---

1 Micheal Macdonagh: *The Speaker of the House* (1914), page 54.

the Chairman of Ways and Means and the Deputy Chairman, who are elected by the House and who may act as Deputy Speaker. But the main burden of the Chair rests upon the Speaker. On almost every morning while the House is sitting he is dealing with a succession of matters important and trivial which need his guidance or decision. Members write, or call in person, to lodge a complaint, ask for assistance on a procedural matter, discuss the course of a debate, and for a dozen other reasons. Numerous "household" matters concerning the management of the Palace of Westminster call for his attention, and there is always a mound of correspondence to be dealt with, to say nothing of his normal constituency work.

THE CLERKS

When Denison was elected to the Chair in 1857—after thirty years in the House—he asked his predecessor, Shaw-Lefevre, whom he should turn to for advice. "No one," Lefevre replied, "you must learn to rely entirely upon yourself." This advice, although excellent for day-to-day conduct in the House, would be fatal if followed literally by a new Speaker. He has at his disposal the accumulated experience and knowledge of the Clerks who sit before him at the Table, and only a particularly stupid man would discard these assets. It was said of Elsynge, Clerk of the House in the middle of the seventeenth century, that "more reverence was paid to his stool than to the Speaker's Chair," and this tribute could have been paid to several of his successors.

The Clerk of the House of Commons is appointed by the Queen on the advice of the Prime Minister. The Clerk-Assistant and Second Clerk-Assistant are appointed on the advice of the Speaker. Until the middle of the seventeenth century there was only one Clerk—in early days a chancery clerk—but the growing realisation of the importance of his office and the increased work of the Commons led to first one, then another, clerk being appointed to assist him. To-day, he has a department of thirty-four.

The principal job of the Clerk used to be to write the Journals of the House, which is a somewhat dry factual account of what the House *decides*.[1] It was the realisation by the House in the seventeenth century that the Journals were of the greatest importance in their forms of debate and procedure which led directly to the elevation of the position of the Clerk from being a mere compiler of the decisions of the House into that of an expert on procedural matters. Hatsell—who held the position from 1768 to 1820—produced an elaborate collection of *Precedents of Proceedings in the House of Commons*, which was replaced by the work of the greatest of all Clerks of the House, Sir Thomas Erskine May, whose *Treatise on the Law, Privilege, Proceedings and Usage of Parliament* has become the text-book of the procedure of Parliament, and which is being constantly revised in the light of changes in procedure. To date it has run through seventeen separate editions. Other Clerks have written books on procedure, but the only book ever written by a Clerk which has achieved a wider fame was Erskine Childers's *The Riddle of the Sands*, which is a classic of its kind, but which has few connections with procedural matters.

The Clerk of the House devotes most of his time to advising the Speaker, and Members, on procedure and the business of the House, and running his own Department. The Journal is the responsibility of the Clerk of the Journals, who has a small department called the Journal Office, which also supervises the publication of the daily *Votes and Proceedings of the House of Commons*, a shorter and simpler version of the Journal and which is published every day when the House is sitting.[2] The Clerk advises the Speaker not only in the House, but whenever questions of procedure or precedent arise. In the House he can lean back in his chair and whisper to the Speaker, or get up and stand beside the Chair. Such hurried discussions do not occur very often, and on at least one occasion it was not of much assistance. Speaker Denison asked the Clerk, Sir Denis le Marchant, when a storm arose in the House, what he advised. "I recommend you, sir, to be very cautious,"

---

1 See Chapter Seven.
2 See Chapter Seven.

the Clerk whispered, and then hurriedly disappeared behind the Chair! At two o'clock every sitting day, the Clerks and the Speaker hold a conference in the Speaker's House, when they go through the business for the day and attempt to foresee any difficulties which may arise. In the case of the Report Stage of a Bill (see Chapter Six) the Speaker is given a marked copy of the amendments, explaining the history of each one—if it was discussed for five hours in Committee and defeated on a division, if the Minister promised to "look at it again," or whatever the circumstances may be—so that he is adequately seized of the implications of each amendment. It is really the job of the Clerks to anticipate difficulties, but it is impossible to do this all the time, and much must be left to the resource, knowledge and authority of the Speaker or, if the House is in Committee, the Chairman.

As well as advising the Chair, the Clerks at the Table record the decisions of the House in Minute books, which are the authority for the *Votes and Proceedings*. Members come to the Table, to "table" Questions or to ask for advice, and frequently they are advised to go to the appropriate department if the matter is specialised. Another Clerk, called the Fourth Clerk at the Table, devotes almost all his time to assisting Commonwealth Parliaments.

There are five small departments under the Clerk. The *Table Office*, consisting of four senior Clerks, is under the control of the Second Clerk-Assistant, and is situated in a tiny room behind the Speaker's Chair. This Office deals principally with Questions and Motions put down by Members, and superintends the printing of the Order Paper of the House in these respects. It is probably the busiest of the five departments when the House is sitting, and its existence—it was created after the last war—is a reflection of the greatly increased number of Questions in recent years, since their burden became too great for the Table to deal with.

The *Public Bill Office*, situated in rooms over the new Chamber of the House, is concerned with all matters in connection with public legislation. In addition to the Clerk of Public Bills and the Clerk of Standing Committees, who are in this office, there are four other Clerks, three of whom are senior Clerks. This office checks Bills, arranges for their printing and re-printing, the publication of amendments to Bills in Committee or on Report, and mans Standing Committees (see Chapter Six).

The *Journal Office*, also situated in rooms over the new House, is responsible for the publication of the daily *Votes and Proceedings of the House of Commons* as well as for the lengthier and more detailed Journal, which is published annually at the end of the Session. This department usually consists of five Clerks.

The *Private Bill Office* is to be found at the end of the Committee Corridor, and overlooks the north corner of the Terrace. This is a very small department, usually consisting of three or four Clerks, and its duties are entirely concerned with the management of Private Business, which includes serving as Clerks to Private Bill Committees.

Next door to the Private Bill Office is the largest of all the departments under the Clerk, the *Committee Office*. It usually consists of nine or ten Clerks, most of whom are senior Clerks, and is under the supervision of the Clerk of Financial and Miscellaneous Committees. The Clerks in the Committee Office are primarily responsible for acting as Clerks to the sub-committees of the Select Committee on Estimates, the Public Accounts Committee, the Committee of Privileges, and the Select Committee on Nationalised Industries (see Chapter Eight). In addition to these responsibilities, the Clerks to the Kitchen, Consolidation Bills, and Statutory Instruments Committees are usually in the Committee Office, and whenever the House established an *ad hoc* Select Committee to examine a particular matter—such as Procedure—one of the Committee Office clerks is appointed to assist it.

As well as working in their specialised fields, four Clerks have to be available throughout the sitting of the House on every week-day to take names in Divisions. One Senior Clerk acts as Secretary to the Chairman of Ways and Means.

The Clerks are servants of the House, paid by the House. They are not Civil Servants (although in matters of salary they are linked to the Civil Service), and this distinction is important. Civil Servants serve the Government; the Clerks serve the House, and are protected by the Privilege of the House when they are acting on its behalf. An attempt to bribe or intimidate an officer of the House in the pursuance of his duty is regarded as an offence as serious as if a Member were involved.

The Clerks also enjoy other exceptional advantages. They are permitted to use almost all of the facilities in the Palace of Westminster available to Members, may enter the Chamber of the House at will when the House is sitting, and can either stand at the Bar, behind the Chair, or use part of the Members' galleries. The impartiality of the Clerks is as important as that of the Speaker, and their discretion must be beyond question, since they hear and see things of the utmost confidence and secrecy. This trust placed in the Officers of the House by Members has never been abused, and the fact that it is taken for granted by Members is the greatest possible compliment which could be paid.

How is a Clerk appointed? He must have a first or second-class degree at University or reach an equivalent standard, and he must pass the Civil Service examinations, as well as receiving the approval of the Clerk of the House himself, who interviews all possible candidates at an early stage. No candidate who fails to receive the Clerk's nomination can go further in the competition, as it is realised that the Clerk alone can judge whether a candidate has the particular qualities needed for such a specialised job. After the Clerk has entered the service of the House, he is moved from one department to another at regular intervals, so that at the end of about fifteen years he has had experience of almost all aspects of the work of the House. If he wants to go to the Table, the vital appointment is that of Second Clerk-Assistant, for he will, in the normal course of events, become Clerk of the House within about fifteen years. This appointment takes place at approximately forty-five years of age, and the unsuccessful aspirants can then decide in which sphere they wish to spend the remainder of their time in the House. Not all Clerks, however, have ambitions for the Table, with its long hours and necessarily late nights, with the consequential dislocation of home life, and many determine upon the field in which they wish to specialise at an earlier time.

Lord Morrison of Lambeth has written an appreciation of the Clerks of the House which may be quoted here.

> I have had a good deal to do with them, and have always found them, whilst quite properly maintaining their independence of the Government and the Opposition, able, courteous, and helpful officers of the House of Commons.[1]

It will be seen that the procedural side of the work of the House is in remarkably few hands, and it is worth noting that although the work of the House has increased tremendously in the past fifty years, the number of Clerks has actually been reduced. It is the duty of the Clerks at all levels to preserve the precedents and the rules of the House; as a result, they frequently have to refuse applications by Members to put down Questions, Motions, or Amendments, and to draw the attention of the Chairman to the fact that a Member is speaking out of order. The Clerks are the servants of the House, not those of individual Members, and it is their responsibility to preserve the rules laid down by the House, and to ensure continuity. It is rare for Members to be in the House for longer than twenty years, but the Clerk of the House and his senior colleagues have far longer experience than this, and whereas the average Member is concerned with his constituency and day-to-day politics, the Clerks are perpetually living with the difficult procedural matters which arise almost daily. The department of the Clerk of the House, although little known outside Westminster, may be said to be one of the most important elements in the continuity and smooth progress of the business of the House of Commons.

THE SERJEANT AT ARMS

The only other non-Members who regularly attend the sittings of the House are the Serjeant at Arms and his two assistants, the

---

1 *Government & Parliament*, page 206.

Deputy and Assistant Serjeants. When the House is sitting, one of them is always on duty in the Serjeant's chair, which is to the right of the Bar, facing the Speaker's Chair, and he wears a court suit of black cloth, with knee-breeches, buckled shoes, and a long sword in a white scabbard. He is noticed by Strangers when he walks up the Floor of the House to move the Mace from on top of the Table to under it when the House resolves itself into Committee, and back again when the Committee becomes the House again. He also carries the Mace on his shoulder in the Speaker's procession every sitting day, and on other ceremonial occasions, as when the House goes to the House of Lords to hear the Queen's Speech or the Royal Assent.

The Serjeant is one of the most important persons concerned with the management of the House of Commons. In the Chamber, apart from his ceremonial functions, he is responsible for assisting the Speaker in the carrying out of his duties; if a Member is rebuked by the Speaker, becomes truculent, and refuses to leave the House when instructed to do so, the Serjeant is ordered to remove the offender; usually a touch on the arm is sufficient, but there have been occasions when the Serjeant and his assistants have had to carry struggling Members out of the Chamber. These disagreeable incidents are very rare, and the intervention of the Serjeant for this duty has not been required for several years.

He is responsible for maintaining order in the lobbies, corridors, and galleries of the House. Numerous doorkeepers and badge messengers, whom he appoints, and who act upon his instructions, carry out this duty in co-operation with the policemen who come from the "A" Division of the Metropolitan Police. Strangers who come to the galleries have to sign a form in which some of the rules of conduct are set out; they may not eat, drink, shout, clap, or make any disturbance; to do so is a contempt of the House, and the offender can be locked up in the Clock Tower until he has "purged his contempt," although usually he is immediately escorted out of the building. From time to time a group of people deliberately plan to interrupt the proceedings of the House by standing up and shouting abuse or slogans, or by throwing pamphlets on to the

Floor of the House. The doorkeepers appear out of nowhere, seize the interrupters, and bustle them unceremoniously out of the gallery.

Trouble can also come from groups of constituents who come to the Central Lobby to see their Member about a grievance, and the police have sometimes to intervene. The police are also responsible for keeping the roads to Westminster clear for Members, and when there is an occasion of extreme political excitement this can be difficult.

The doorkeepers are carefully chosen by the Serjeant, and are almost invariably ex-servicemen. They wear full evening dress when the House is sitting, and fulfil many duties, from tracking down Members with messages to assisting the Serjeant when trouble occurs either in the House or in the lobbies.

The Serjeant and his two deputies are responsible, under the Speaker, for the domestic arrangements of the House, and for the supervision of the employees of the Ministry of Works—mostly cleaners—who work in the precincts of the House. It is to him that many complaints are directed by Members and officials about accommodation and equipment. Some Members find it very curious that these responsibilities should be held by someone who is not a Member, and from time to time an agitation arises for a Committee of the House to be appointed to manage the affairs of the House which are under the control of the Serjeant. But as the system has worked extremely satisfactorily since 1812, it seems unlikely that the House would alter it.

When the House is sitting there is a stream of Members going to the Serjeant's Chair; observant Strangers see him speaking to them, and then writing on a buff form, stamping it with a curiously-shaped machine, and handing the form to the Member, who immediately leaves the Chamber. The Serjeant is distributing admission orders to special galleries for friends or constituents of Members, and the stamp is an ingenious one which stamps the exact time when the order was issued. If the galleries are full, the Serjeant will quietly explain the fact to the Member, but usually the galleries begin to empty at about five o'clock, and Members are able to get tickets from the Serjeant.

In a phrase, the Serjeant is the executive officer of the House, responsible for maintaining order in the precincts of the House, and for arresting or summoning persons who have offended against the House and who have been ordered to appear before it at the Bar. On these occasions the Serjeant stands at the Bar, beside the offender, with the Mace over his shoulder, as the symbol of the authority of the House.

CHAPTER FIVE

The Parliamentary Day

From Mondays to Thursdays in a normal week when Parliament is in session, the House of Commons meets at half past two in the afternoon and adjourns at half past ten in the evening; on Fridays, it meets at eleven o'clock in the morning, and rises at half past four in the afternoon. The principal business before the House must be concluded by ten p.m. from Mondays to Thursdays, and at four o'clock on Fridays: there is then a half-hour debate on the motion for the Adjournment of the House, in which a Member raises a matter in which he is interested, and to which a responsible Minister makes a brief reply.

These times for the sittings of the House are laid down by the *Standing Orders*, which are simply the written regulations of the House. They are not a code of procedure, for most of the business of the House is governed by precedent and the common sense of the Chair. The Standing Orders relating to public business[1] lay down the minimum amount of rules and restrict the previous practice of the House; they form the skeleton, as it were, of the procedure of the House. If the times of meeting are to be altered, then the House must pass a motion to suspend the appropriate Standing Order, of which printed notice must be given. Thus, if Standing Order Number One (Sittings of the House) is suspended, the House can sit all night if need be; but there are some items of business—for example, the Finance Bill and the Consolidated Fund

---

1 Private Bills have their own Standing Orders.

Bill, as they originated in a Resolution of the Committee of Ways and Means—which are automatically "exempted business," which means that the "Ten o'clock Rule" does not apply in their cases.

The Palace of Westminster resembles a small town in the complexity and variety of the people who work and live there. At about seven o'clock in the morning the town begins to come to life. A small army of cleaners arrive and begin to prepare the Palace for the day's work. Post office vans speed into New Palace Yard and deposit a mound of post which is sent to a large sorting room, where the staff collect the mail for Members into separate bundles for collection. Other vans and lorries drive into the courtyards with food for the refreshment department, Parliamentary papers for the Vote Office,[1] oil fuel for the central heating unit, and for a hundred other purposes. The policemen and custodians who have been on duty all night are relieved by the new shift, and by nine o'clock some of the doorkeepers and other officials are arriving. Stationery is being laid out on desks in the Library and writing-rooms for Members; technicians may be working on lights or microphones which have been giving trouble in the Chamber; the Houses of Parliament telephone exchange starts to receive and dispatch calls.

By half past nine the cleaners have left the lobbies, rooms and corridors, and the permanent staff of the two Houses of Parliament are arriving. Doorkeepers in their full evening dress and gold badge on their white shirt-fronts are in the Members' Lobby; some Members' secretaries are hurrying in, and here and there a Member is arriving. By ten o'clock, even on a Monday, there is a pleasant atmosphere of vitality about the place.

Our Member is one of the early arrivals. He parks his car in New Palace Yard, walks into the Members' entrance, and down a corridor which runs beside Westminster Hall. He leaves his hat and coat in what were the old cloisters of St. Stephen's Chapel, and climbs up a wide and ornate staircase into another short corridor, which leads to some steps and thence into the Members'

---

1 A little office in the Members' Lobby, which distributes Parliamentary papers to Members and Officers of the House.

Lobby. To the left of the entrance, just off the Lobby, is the Members' Post Office. He goes into this, and asks for his post. The clerk on duty calls into a microphone, "Mr. Smith, please;" there is a clatter, and a little lift, sent from the sorting room, arrives with our Member's post neatly tied up with a rubber band.

It is now half past ten, and the Palace is alive with Members, officials and messengers. If a Standing Committee is meeting, the Members' Tea Room is a busy place from ten o'clock until twenty-five minutes past, when the Members of the Committee gulp down the last dregs of their coffee, seize their bundles of post, and hasten upstairs to the Committee Corridor to find where their Committee is meeting. Other Members who are more fortunate arrive at their leisure throughout the morning, and attend to their correspondence, do some research in the Library, or talk politics with their friends.

Standing Committees meet on Tuesdays, Wednesdays, and Thursdays from ten-thirty to one o'clock. In the Committee Corridor there will be found several Members dictating letters to their secretaries, preparing speeches, drinking coffee, or talking to colleagues or officials. Whenever the door into the Committee Room is opened, the faithful few inside hear a sudden cheerful roar of conversation, as instantly silenced by the closing of the door. Our Member has been sitting dutifully in his place for an hour or so, reading his correspondence, and making notes for his replies. He has little interest in the Bill under discussion, but he has been appointed to the Committee as a Government supporter, and the Whip in charge of his party in the Committee is very strict about attendance. At length he slips down to where the Whip is sitting, and, in a whisper, asks if he can safely leave. The Whip counts his supporters, and replies that he can go into the corridor but must stay there for the time being, as a division is expected soon. Our Member, clutching his unanswered post, bows to the Chairman and walks happily out of the room, ignoring the jibe of an opponent about "the *remarkable* interest shown in this Bill by the members of the party opposite."

After he has been in the corridor for a few minutes, enjoying his coffee and dealing with his letters, the policemen and doorkeepers suddenly bawl, "Division in Number Twelve," and several Members rush off in the direction of Committee Room Twelve. Our Member's Committee is meeting in Room Ten, so he continues his reading for a short time before the peace is again broken by shouts of "Count in Number Ten." The Whip has let too many of his supporters leave the room; a wily member of the Opposition has counted the numbers of Members left and has persuaded some of his colleagues to walk out; the Clerk has whispered to the Chairman, and the discussion on the Bill has come to an end for the moment as there is no quorum present.[1] The Government supporters pour back into the room to derisive cheers from the Opposition, and the proceedings are resumed. Our Member is trapped; the Whip is glaring round at his flock, almost daring them to ask him for permission to go, he has had a black look from the Minister for losing the quorum, and he is not going to risk it happening again.

At one o'clock the Chairman adjourns the meeting of the Committee, and our liberated Member goes to have lunch. If he eats in the building he has a choice of the Members' Tea Room, where he can have a cold snack, the Members' Cafeteria, where he can have a hot snack, or the Members' Dining Room, where a full lunch is served.

Mr. Speaker, wearing his court dress, but not yet wigged and gowned, meets the Clerks at the Table in his Library at two o'clock. The Clerks are also in their official uniform, and the purpose of the meeting is to run through the business set down for that day and to try and anticipate any difficulties which may arise. The Government has just decided to send a battalion of troops to one of the Colonies, where there has been trouble. A member of the Opposition has asked the Speaker if he can ask a *Private Notice Question* to the Secretary of State for War. This is a procedure which is used when a Member wishes to ask a Question of urgent importance of which it has not been possible to give written notice beforehand, since the news has only just come through. This is almost invariably the case if there has been an aeroplane or railway accident. If the Speaker is convinced that the matter is really urgent,

1 See Glossary, page 154.

and if the question was brought to his attention before twelve o'clock (midday), he can allow it to be asked at the end of Question Time. He has decided to do so in this case; the Clerk warns him that the Member may try to move the Adjournment of the House "on a definite matter of urgent public importance" if he is not satisfied by the reply of the Minister. If the Speaker accepts the Motion, it must be debated on the same evening at seven o'clock, so he must at least begin to make up his mind in advance. Is the matter *definite*, or is it based merely upon an uncorroborated report in the newspapers? Is it *urgent*, so that the House must debate it *now*, rather than to-morrow? Is it *important*? It is a serious thing for the Speaker to accept such a Motion, for it completely disrupts the business set down for that day.

At about twenty-five past two the Speaker's Procession sets out from the Speaker's House for the Chamber. It consists of a senior doorkeeper, who leads it; the Serjeant at Arms bearing the Mace; Mr. Speaker, whose long robe is carried by his Train-bearer; his Secretary and Chaplain. The Speaker's House is in fact about two minutes' leisurely walk from the Chamber, but the Procession goes along the corridors next to the Library to the Lower Waiting Hall, then into the Central Lobby, and thence down the short corridor into the Members' Lobby and the House. It is regarded by visitors as one of the great Parliamentary ceremonies, and it is carried out with some pomp and dignity. In the Central Lobby the Inspector of Police calls out "Hats off, Str-a-a-ngers!" and all the policemen and any male Strangers who are hatted stand bareheaded until the procession has passed, while all Members and Officers bow to Mr. Speaker as he passes on his way to the House.

In the Chamber itself, Members are gathering for Prayers. The Galleries are empty, and the three chairs for the Clerks in front of the Speaker's Chair have been removed, and two kneeling-stools are in their places. As the procession comes slowly down the corridors and enters the Members' Lobby, the Head Doorkeeper advances to the Bar of the House and calls out "Sp-ee-ak-err!" Members rise to their feet as the Speaker, the Chaplain, and the Serjeant enter. The trio bow deeply at the Bar towards the Chair, advance up the Floor, bow again, and then, after the Speaker and the Chaplain have reached their places, they bow once more. The Serjeant places the Mace on the Table, and the Chaplain begins to read the prayers. It is an old Parliamentary joke that he looks at the Members and prays for the country.

When Prayers, which last about five minutes, are over, the Speaker takes the Chair, the kneeling-stools are removed, and the Clerks take their places at the Table. The doors to the Gallery are opened, and Strangers start to pour into the Galleries. After a moment or two, when everyone has settled himself, the Speaker stands up, calls out, "Order! Order!" and the business of the day begins. The very first item may be a reply from the Queen to an Address presented by the House. This is conveyed by one of the Whips who has an honorary position in the Royal Household; he advances up the Floor from the Bar, bowing deeply, and carrying a white wand which looks exactly like a billiard-cue. In front of the Mace he halts, and reads the Queen's Message; and then, again bowing, he retreats backwards until he reaches the Bar.

If any Member wishes to present a *Petition* to the House, this is the time to do it. Rules for Petitions are strict, and are supervised by the Committee on Public Petitions, to which all Petitions are referred. Before the Petition is ever presented to the House it is inspected by the Journal Office (see page 57) to make sure that it is in order. The Member must then enter his Petition in a list in the Table Office (see page 56) and he will be told on which day he can present it. The Member rises in his place and informs the House that he wishes to present a Petition signed by so many of his constituents, or people in a certain area (Members are not obliged to present petitions signed by their own constituents if they disagree with their terms) concerning such-and-such a matter, and ends, "And Your Petitioners, as in duty bound, will ever pray." The Member can ask that the Clerk should read the Petition, but he usually does this himself. The Petition is then carried to the Chair and put in a green bag hanging at the back of it. Apart from the Report from the Committee on Public Petitions, this is almost certainly the last that will ever be heard about the Petition.

The first item on the Order Paper is *Private Business*. This is not a discussion on the internal affairs of the House, but the time allocated for the Private Bills (see Chapter Six) which have been put down for their next stages by the Promoters. The Speaker says, "The Clerk will now proceed to read the titles of the Private Bills set down for consideration this day," and the Clerk, rising to his feet, reads out the titles on the Order Paper. If no Member cries "Object!" each bill is declared to have passed that stage, second reading, consideration, third reading, as the case may be. Private business must end by a quarter to three, but it is very unusual for it to take more than a few minutes. The House then proceeds to *Questions*, which last until half past three.[1]

QUESTION TIME

Members may put down Questions to Ministers only about matters for which they are responsible to Parliament. A Member must give notice of his Question in writing either at the Table or in the Table Office (see page 56); if he wants an oral answer he puts a "star" against it, and two clear days' notice must be given, to enable the Department concerned to prepare an answer. Thus, if the Member wants to ask a Question on Thursday, he must hand it in to the Table on Monday, and it will be printed on the Tuesday morning as one of the Questions to be asked on Thursday. If the Member only wants a *written* answer—as, for example, if he wants to know some detailed facts and figures—there is not the same degree of urgency, and it is usually several days before the reply is printed in *Hansard* (see page 113). No Member is allowed to put down more than two Questions for oral answer on one day.

Questions to Ministers are surrounded with complicated rules, which it is the duty of the Clerks to see are strictly followed. A Question must seek information or press for action; it may not suggest its own answer, and cannot be argumentative or hypothetical;

---

1 Normally there are no Questions on Fridays. The House meets at eleven o'clock, and after Prayers and any Ministerial statements, proceeds immediately to the Orders of the Day or Motions.

the subject of the Question must be within the responsibility of the Minister. There are other rules, but these are the most important. It is sometimes very difficult to decide where a Minister's responsibilities begin and end, and if the Member is dissatisfied with the ruling of the Clerks he can appeal to the Speaker; this happens fairly often, but it is unusual for the Speaker to overrule the Clerks. It is not usually realised that a Minister is not obliged to answer any Question put down to him; it is a matter of courtesy for him to do so, but obviously a Minister who refused to answer Questions— except on rare occasions when it is felt that it is not in the public interest for certain information, (on Defence, for example), to be published—would get a hot reception from the House.

Our Member has received letters from several of his constituents, complaining about a dangerous corner of the main road in a village in his constituency; there have been several accidents at this corner, and his constituents are anxious that traffic-lights should be put there, or something else done to reduce the chances of further accidents. The Member can write personally to the Minister, or put down a Question; some Members always put down Questions at once, others content themselves with a letter, with a Question in mind if the Minister refuses his request. Our Member has received a polite answer to his letter, regretting that the Minister cannot do anything at the moment. The Member thinks this is not good enough, so he writes out a Question on a piece of paper.

> Mr. Smith. To ask the Minister of Transport, if he will reconsider, on humanitarian grounds, his extraordinary decision not to authorise steps to reduce the danger of accidents at Hagley Corner, where twenty-seven people have been seriously injured in the past eight months.

The Member then trots along to the Table Office, and hands his suggested question to one of the Clerks, who scrutinises it carefully. The Minister of Transport, like all Ministers, answers questions on specified days worked out on a "roster" system and announced well in advance, and the Member has just missed one of these, and will have to wait for a week. Does he still want an oral answer? Yes, he does. The Clerk puts a star by the Question. The Clerk suggests that the remark about "humanitarian grounds" and the description of the Minister's decision as "extraordinary" should be omitted, as they are both unnecessary and possibly argumentative, and that the wording of the Question could be improved so that the Minister will know exactly what the Member is getting at. They confer for a short time, and then produce a new draft, which contains all the information in two Questions.

* Mr. Smith (*Snodsbury*). To ask the Minister of Transport, if he is aware of the fact that twenty-seven people have been seriously injured at Hagley Corner in the village of Betterpass, and what steps he proposes to take to reduce the danger to life at this corner.
* Mr. Smith (*Snodsbury*). To ask the Minister of Transport, if he will reconsider his decision not to authorise the erection of traffic-lights at Hagley Corner, in the village of Betterpass.

The Member having approved this version, the Clerk puts the paper with the two Questions written on it in a special tray which will later be collected by a messenger and sent to be printed.

On the following morning the Questions appear as two of many which have been tabled the previous day for the next Ministry of Transport day, and at the Ministry the Hagley Corner file is dug out. The Civil Servants examine it, and prepare a draft reply for the Minister. In the case of an oral Question, the original Question is not usually difficult to answer, but Members are allowed at least one "supplementary" Question after the Minister has replied, and it is the task of the Civil Servants to try to anticipate this "supplementary." From Mr. Smith's original letter to the Minister they have a pretty good idea of the line he is likely to take, so they prepare a short list of facts which may help the Minister. The draft Answers which go before the Minister might read as follows.

I will, with permission, answer these two Questions together. I regret that I cannot at the moment alter my decision on this matter, but discussions are continuing with the Betterpass Rural Council and officials of my Ministry to see if an alternative method of reducing the dangers of this corner can be found.

Facts for Supplementaries: Of the twenty-seven injuries in the past eight months, only one (to an old woman) was serious; most of them were caused to children running out of Hagley Corner School at four o'clock in the evening; a school warden has now been appointed to supervise the orderly crossing of the road by the children.

The corner is already a bottle-neck for traffic, and lights would cause a serious delay to through traffic.

The corner has been widened twice in the past year, and new "Danger" signs have been put up.

Armed with these facts, the Minister goes to the House on the day when his department has Questions, while Mr. Smith polishes up his withering supplementary.

The Questions are printed in numerical order, Ministry by Ministry, and the Speaker calls out the name of the Member who has put the Question down. The Member bobs up, says "Question Number, Sir," and the Minister reads out his reply. Supplementaries may then be allowed and when the Speaker decides that enough time has been taken over that Question, he calls the Member who has put down the next.

Mr. Smith's Questions are numbered 37 and 38, and at about ten minutes past three he is beginning to wonder if they will be reached. The Secretary of State for Scotland is in difficulties with Scottish Members on the subject of Scottish unemployment, and supplementaries are coming thick and fast from both sides. Eventually his ordeal is over, and the Minister of Transport and his Under-Secretary move along the Treasury Bench to their places opposite the Dispatch Box. The Minister's *Parliamentary Private Secretary*, a back-bench Member who acts as his unpaid assistant in the House, sits behind him; he has a copy of the answers, and he is ready to dart to the Civil Servants grouped uncomfortably in the officials' box under the Press Gallery for information if the Minister gets into difficulties.

At twenty past three Question 37 is reached. Mr. Speaker calls "Mr. Smith"; "Question Number 37, Sir," our Member says. The Minister advances to the Dispatch Box and reads out his prepared answer, which has been slightly altered.

> I will, with permission, answer Questions 37 and 38 together. I am fully aware of the dangerous condition of this corner, and although I very much regret that I am unable to change my decision not to authorise the erection of traffic-lights, discussions are taking place between officials of my Ministry and representatives of the local authorities concerned to see what can be done to reduce the danger to life at this corner.

Mr. Smith leaps up to fire off his "supplementary."

> While thanking my Right Hon. Friend for the latter part of his Answer, is he aware that this is an extremely urgent matter involving the safety of many of my constituents, and that while these discussions are going on there may be more accidents at this corner, one of which may be fatal?

The Minister replies:

> I am indeed aware of the urgency of this matter, but, to put the facts into their proper perspective I think I should inform my Hon. Friend that most of the accidents have involved children running out of Hagley Corner School, and that the provision of a warden to prevent this happening has already greatly improved matters. We are anxious to deal with the problem once and for all, but neither the local authorities nor the Ministry feel that traffic-lights would be the best solution. We have widened the corner twice in the past year, and have put

new "Danger" signs into position, so I do not think that we can be accused of indifference to this problem.

"Mr. Robinson," the Speaker calls, and Mr. Robinson rises to ask Question 39. The series of events which began with a letter to our Member and has ended with a Question in the House, may not yet be over. If the Member was dissatisfied with the answer he could have jumped up on a point of order and given notice that "in view of the unsatisfactory nature of that reply, I will raise the matter on the Adjournment at the earliest possible opportunity." The Member would then "ballot" for the opportunity of having a half-hour Adjournment debate at the end of a future sitting day, and if successful, could initiate a short debate on the subject of Hagley Corner.

Question Time ends at half past three; all Questions which have not been answered orally by then will receive written replies, which are published in the day's *Hansard*. If a Member really wants his oral answer so that he can ask a damaging supplementary, he can postpone his Question before half past three, so that it will come up on another day.

Question Time usually sees the House at its most lively, with the benches and galleries crowded, and with all the great Parliamentary figures of the day in attendance. The process of question and answer is a good test of a Minister's ability, since he can be faced with some very nasty and unexpected supplementaries. He may say that such-and-such has always been part of Her Majesty's Government's policy; the Opposition front bench spokesman jumps to his feet and triumphantly asks why it was that one of the Minister's senior Cabinet colleagues had said in a speech at Great Twittering in 1953 that the very idea of such a policy was repugnant to his party. A Minister faced with this horrible quandary will have to answer swiftly; he may content himself with the lofty "I fail to see what that has to do with this Question, Mr. Speaker," or the sarcastic, "The Hon. Member is, as always, preoccupied with the distant past, while we on this side of the House are more concerned with the future," or he can try to prove that his Right Honourable Friend had never said anything of the sort, or was quoted out of context, or had never meant what was inferred from his remarks, or had been right to say it *at the time*. In any event, the issue must be faced there and then in the House, and it is a great test of a Minister; the House is listening eagerly to see how he will get himself out of the mess; the Opposition are vigilant and gleeful; one false word might start a Parliamentary storm, with Members bobbing up with penetrating questions or points of order and the Speaker frequently on his feet giving complicated rulings.

When Questions are over at half past three, the Member who has been allowed to ask his "private notice question" does so, and the Minister answers it; supplementaries are allowed for a while, but the Chair does not usually allow the exchanges to go on for very long, as there is no motion before the House, and the proceedings are therefore informal. At this time Ministers may make statements about changes in policy by their departments, and questions from Members will follow. If there has just been a by-election, the new Member stands at the Bar with two Members, one on either side, as "sponsors." After the statements and questions are over, the Speaker says, "Members desiring to take their seats will come to the Table," and the trio advance from the Bar, bowing three times. The Clerk of the House is waiting at the Government Dispatch Box, and the new Member hands him a long piece of blue paper prepared by the Public Bill Office which is in effect a receipt for the Writ, showing that the Returning Officer has sent it to the Clerk to the Crown, who has informed the Public Bill Office. The Member then takes the Oath, standing by the Dispatch Box, and signs the roll on the Table; the Clerk then introduces him to Mr. Speaker, with whom he shakes hands before walking past the Chair. If the Member has won, or held, a marginal seat, every stage in his introduction is loudly cheered by his party colleagues, and cheerful cries of "resign" are hurled at the defeated party.

After this, the time has come for any Member who wishes to ask for leave to move the Adjournment of the House "on a matter of urgent public importance" under Standing Order Number Nine.

As has been explained above, the decision whether leave shall be given lies entirely with the Speaker, and if he decides in favour of the motion, and forty Members rise to support the application, the debate will begin at seven o'clock. If Mr. Speaker decides against the motion, there are usually a few minutes of points of order when Members, "with the greatest possible respect" try to persuade the Speaker that he should accept it.

After this has been disposed of, statements may be made by senior Ministers and other Members in commemoration of distinguished Members who have just died. Then, if it is a Wednesday, there may be a ballot for *Private Members' Motions*. Members can put their names down against numbers in a book which is kept in the "No" Lobby from two-fifteen until half past three under the supervision of Clerks from the Public Bill Office; slips of paper corresponding to the numbers are put in a large black dispatch box which is sent to the Table. At the appropriate time Mr. Speaker says, "Ballot for Private Members' Motions for—"(naming a future day allocated at the beginning of the session for Private Members' Motions). He is handed the book with the Members' signatures, and the Clerk-Assistant opens the ballot box and produces one of the slips of paper. "Number" he calls out; Mr. Speaker consults his book, and calls the Member who has his name against that number. The Member rises, and says, "I beg to give notice that on—, I shall call attention to . . ., and move a Resolution"; the same procedure is used for two more Members, so that three Motions will be on the Order Paper for that particular day, although probably only the first one will be debated.

When this is over, and the black dispatch box has been removed from the Clerk's desk, any Member or Minister may make a brief personal statement to the House. These statements, which cannot be debated, are usually made by Ministers who have resigned from the Government as a result of a disagreement on policy. Sometimes one is made by a back-bench Member who may have been involved in a disagreeable case in the Law Courts, or has been accused by the Press or another Member of doing something he did not do, or desires to apologise for a mistake on his part, or for something he had said or done.

Questions of *Privilege* can then be raised; this is the most convenient time for doing this, but in fact there have been instances when the ordinary business of the House has been interrupted to bring the matter to the immediate attention of the Speaker. It is the job of the Speaker to decide if what is called a *"prima facie"* case has been made, in other words, to rule if, in his opinion, the Member has raised a justified complaint. If he does so rule, the matter is committed at once to the Committee of Privileges (see Chapter Eight).

Public Bills are then presented (see page 85) and any Government motions about the business of the House then follow, and then, last of all, motions for introducing Bills under the "Ten-minute Rule" (see page 101).

All this takes a long time to describe, for almost every possible proceeding has been mentioned. On a usual Parliamentary day, Private Business takes only a few minutes, Questions run until half past three, a statement by a Minister follows, a couple of Public Bills are introduced, a Government motion on the sittings of the House is passed "on the nod" (that is, without a Division) and the main business of the day is entered upon at about a quarter to four.

The business before the House is that which has been put down by the Government, which has the control of almost all Parliamentary time except for certain days—most Fridays and an occasional Wednesday—set aside for Private Members. The business may be a stage of an important Bill or a debate on a Motion for the Adjournment of the House formally moved by the Government Chief Whip. Subjects like Foreign Policy are often debated on such Motions. Unless there is a motion put down as first business the Speaker says, "The Clerk will now proceed to read the Orders of the Day," and the Clerk reads out the title of the first Order, and the cry "Orders of the Day" rings down the corridors.

While the debate is continuing in the House, a considerable amount of parliamentary and political activity will be going on in other parts of the Palace. Both political parties have party committees on such specialised subjects as Science, Trade and Industry and Foreign Affairs, and these meet in Committee rooms of the House in the afternoon. Although these are not strictly Parliamentary committees, they have become extremely important in recent years, and are usually well attended.

Select Committees of the House may also be meeting in other Committee Rooms, and a Private Bill Committee may be concluding its proceedings. There is usually a small crowd of Members beside the ticker-tape machine in the corridor next to the Smoking Room to see the latest news. Other Members are roused from whatever they are doing by receiving a "green card" from one of the badge messengers, which tells him that a friend or constituent would like to see him in the Central Lobby. Some Members are entertaining guests, and in the summer tea on the Terrace is very popular with visitors. The Library is always busy, and in the interview and writing-rooms other Members are dictating or writing letters, or preparing speeches. A stream of Members is going into the Table Office to put down Questions or Motions or ask for advice. The whole building resembles a vast beehive, with constant movement and noise.

If the normal "Ten o'clock Rule" is in operation, the principal business for the day must end at that hour. If a motion to suspend the Standing Order has been put down by the Government it is moved just before ten o'clock, and the Opposition can divide on the Question. If there is still a Member speaking at ten o'clock, and there is no suspension motion, the debate will be automatically adjourned unless the Closure[1] is claimed, accepted by the Chair, and agreed to by the House. After the division (if any) on this is over, and the Closure is carried, the "main Question," that is, the Question the House was debating before the Closure was claimed, is put at once, and the House can come to a decision.

The last item is the half-hour Adjournment Debate which has already been mentioned in this chapter. Members ballot for the chance of raising subjects on the Adjournment, and even if the

1 See Glossary, page 139.

House sits all night the half-hour Adjournment debate is held. These debates are usually very intimate and quite friendly, with only a handful of interested Members in the Chamber. After half an hour the Speaker interrupts the proceedings—if there is still a Member on his feet—and the House is automatically adjourned. The Serjeant at Arms advances up the Floor of the House, seizes the Mace, puts it on his shoulder and walks out of the Chamber through the door behind the Chair. The Speaker, who has left the Chair and is waiting behind it for the Serjeant to pass, then walks out of the House behind him. The Serjeant halts in the Speaker's Lobby, and Mr. Speaker says to him as he passes, "Usual time to-morrow" (or "to-day" if the House has sat after midnight, or "Monday" if it is a Friday), the Serjeant repeats the information to the Head Doorkeeper who announces the news in the Members' Lobby. Down the corridors the cry of "Who Goes Home?" is raised as soon as the House rises. This is a reminder of the times when Members went home in escorted groups for fear of brigands on the roads. Then comes the cry, "Usual time to-morrow," and the lights are switched off, with the exception of a few single bulbs in the main corridors, the light over Big Ben, which shines[1] while the House is sitting also goes out, and after half an hour or so the ghostly Palace is left to the care of the lonely policemen and custodians who patrol it through the night. The Parliamentary Day is over.

---

1 In Victorian times this light only shone in the direction of the West End of London, it being assumed that Members only inhabited this part of the city!

CHAPTER SIX

An Act is Passed

Legislation—the passing of Acts of Parliament—is perhaps the most important of Parliament's many tasks, and in this process the House of Commons occupies the most influential position. To become an Act of Parliament, and thereby part of the law of the land, a Bill must pass through both Houses of Parliament and then receive the Royal Assent. The Royal Assent has not been withheld for over two hundred and fifty years, and its granting has become a complete formality. For practical purposes, the House of Lords cannot reject a money Bill,[1] and can only hold up a Bill for a year, so that the real power in legislation lies with the House of Commons.

Generally speaking, Bills fall into one of two categories. *Public Bills* affect everyone; *Private Bills* are promoted by local authorities, companies, and even individuals, and only concern a limited number of people. Thus, a Bill to enable the Government to acquire all meadows in Great Britain would be a Public Bill; a Bill to empower a Borough Council to acquire all meadows in its area would be a Private Bill. Most Public Bills are promoted by the Government, but some are presented by private Members of Parliament—backbenchers—and these are known as *Private Members' Bills*. There are occasions when it is difficult to determine whether a Bill is a public or private one, in which case the Speaker has to make the decision, and from time to time Bills are presented which incorporate

---

1 See footnote to page 2.

matters of public and private interest. These are known as *Hybrid Bills*, but need not concern us here.

The process of legislation is so complicated that it is difficult to describe it briefly, but taking some entirely imaginary examples, it is possible to see in broad outlines how the machinery works. As the procedures for Public and Private Bills are different, we will take them separately.

PUBLIC BILLS

We will assume that the Government decide to pass an Act which forbids shops opening after five o'clock in the evening. Perhaps the political party which forms the Government has decided to adopt this policy and has put it in its election manifesto at a General Election, or it may be that it has decided that such legislation has become necessary for various reasons. The matter of *policy* is decided by the Cabinet, and the appropriate Minister—in this case the Home Secretary—is instructed by the Cabinet to prepare a Bill on these broad lines. He then informs his permanent Civil Servants at his Ministry, who start to prepare the proposed Bill. At a very early stage a Parliamentary Draftsman is brought into the discussions. This official, an experienced lawyer, is responsible for writing the Bill and he takes charge of it until it receives the Royal Assent. His position is an extremely important one, for when the Bill becomes an Act, it must be interpreted in the Law Courts, and there must not be any loopholes through which a clever lawyer might extricate a client who had offended against the new law. The Bill cannot merely say, "After five o'clock in the evening no shop may remain open;" all those Acts which say that they can remain open must be repealed—in other words, ended—and a list of penalties for failure must be set out; then the question would arise, what is a "shop?" The phrase must be carefully defined, for the owner of a stall in a market, for example, might claim that he is not a "shop," and the possibilities are limitless. Is a garage a "shop?" The Bill must state what exactly a shop is; when it must close; what will happen if the shopkeeper breaks the law; what old Acts are repealed, and so on. If an Act of Parliament is so loosely drafted that a clever man can "drive a horse and cart" through the law, the reputation of Parliament will fall in the eyes of the citizen, and respect for the law is the foundation of society.

But the Minister's troubles are only just beginning. His Civil Servants may point out—and it is their duty to warn the Minister against trying to pass an unworkable Bill which will be useless and injure the Government—that chemists' shops should be exempted, at least for an hour, to enable people to purchase drugs and medical equipment after they have come from doctors' surgeries, most of which are from six to seven in the evening. And then, what about tobacconists? Are they to be excluded from opening at a time when they do most of their business? And food shops? Are these to close at five o'clock? The Minister has to take away these problems and think them over, and perhaps discuss them informally with his colleagues. Perhaps he is convinced that chemists should be allowed to stay open until seven o'clock to serve customers who have doctors' prescriptions which have to be made up. For such a change in the *policy* of his Bill he will have to return to the Cabinet for approval. He will ask for the matter to be put down on the Agenda for a meeting of the Cabinet, and when the item is reached the Prime Minister will ask him to raise the matter, which the Minister should do as briefly as possible. If the Cabinet agree that the exemption is a fair one, he can return to his Civil Servants and tell them to re-draft the Bill accordingly.

On such an important Bill there will be many conferences at the Ministry, at which various problems will be raised and thrashed out. At length the draft Bill is finished, and is privately printed for the use of a very limited number of officials and members of the Government. It must be assumed by the Cabinet that the Minister has carried out the task entrusted to him, but there may be some further points of detail on which some Cabinet members are unhappy. How can a check be kept upon chemists to make sure that they are not selling items not on a doctor's prescription? Will the new law encourage doctors to put things on prescriptions to enable their patients to go to chemists in the evenings? And then perhaps the vexed subject of tobacconists and food shops comes up again. Will the new law make the Government more unpopular with the ordinary citizen than is necessary?

At length the draft Bill is approved, and discussions take place as to when it should be presented to Parliament. The year's "time-table" has to be prepared very carefully, to make sure that there is plenty of time for all the Government legislation to get through. We will assume that our Bill's programme is as follows:

(1) Presented in the House of Commons[1] on 10th November and printed on the same day.
(2) To be read a second time on 18th November and to be sent "upstairs" to a Standing Committee.
(3) To come out of Committee by the middle of February.
(4) To have the Report Stage in the first fortnight of March, and to be read a third time a week later.
(5) To be read a second time in the House of Lords in the first week of April.
(6) To return to the Commons in the first week in May.
(7) To receive the Royal Assent before the Whitsun Recess.
(8) The new Act to become operative on 1st September.

In the Speech from the Throne the Queen makes reference to the fact that "an important measure for limiting the hours of opening of shops will be laid before you," but it is unlikely that this will be the first that has been heard of the proposal, particularly if the political party which forms the Government has been promising to provide legislation on this subject. If the Opposition party is opposed to shorter hours of opening for shops—probably on the ground that this will cause unnecessary inconvenience to the general public and mean less profits for shop-owners—their spokesmen will criticise the proposal in general terms in the debate

---

1 Some Government Bills—but seldom as controversial as this—are introduced in the House of Lords.

on the Address.[1] This is the opening debate of a new Session, and immediately follows the State Opening of Parliament. By tradition two back-benchers on the Government side—one of whom is often a new Member—move and second the motion that "an Humble Address be presented to Her Majesty," thanking her for the Gracious Speech. They are followed by the Leader of the Opposition and the Prime Minister in turn, and the ensuing debate lasts for several days, in the course of which the Opposition will probably move amendments regretting that the Gracious Speech did not refer to such-and-such, or contain proposals for this-and-that. The opening day of the debate is a grand Parliamentary occasion, following, as it does, all the pomp of the State Opening in the Lords.

The controversy over our Bill will now begin in earnest in the Press as well as at Westminster. Government spokesmen will support the proposal, pointing out that shop-workers have to work too long, and that by shortening their hours no real harm would be inflicted upon the public, and so on.

The draft Bill will be in the hands of the Public Bill Office for some time before presentation, when the Clerk of Public Bills will examine it to see that it complies with the rules of the House. He takes particular care to see that the contents of the Bill are covered by the title and that the forms and procedure which are necessary if the Bill involves a charge on public funds have been followed. If the Bill does not comply with these rules, the attention of the Draftsman is called to the omission when the Bill is in draft form, but if it has been actually presented and "ordered to be printed" the matter is reported to the Speaker, who may order the Bill to be withdrawn. The Office will be warned of the time of publication of the Bill, and will inform the Stationery Office—who print the Bill—of these arrangements. On the day before presentation the Public Bill Office is informed, and a Notice of Presentation is put upon the Order Paper of the House. This appears after the list of Questions and before the Orders of the Day.

---

1 In fact the Government usually "give notice" of the Bill before this debate to prevent it being discussed, but we will assume that they have not done so on this occasion.

NOTICE(S) OF PRESENTATION OF BILL(S)

The Home Secretary[1]

SHOPS (HOURS OF OPENING); Bill to regulate the hours of opening of shops; and for other purposes connected therewith.

The Bill is laid upon the Table by the Public Bill Office in "dummy" form; this is a piece of buff paper with the titles of the Bill and the names of the Members who support it. These supporters, in the case of a Government Bill, will be the other Ministers who are involved in the operation of the Bill, and their names will be printed on the back of the printed Bill.

After Questions the Speaker will stand up and call the Home Secretary by name; this gentleman, sitting on the Treasury Bench, will nod towards the Chair; "Shops (Hours of Opening) Bill," the Clerk says, reading from the "dummy" Bill; "Second Reading, what day?" inquires the Speaker; "To-morrow, sir," one of the Whips replies. By this brief process the Bill is ordered to have been read a first time and to be printed, and the fact will be recorded in the *Votes and Proceedings*. In many cases the Bill will have been printed already, and bundles—still sealed—placed in the Vote Office. As soon as the House has ordered the Bill to be printed the Public Bill office informs the Vote Office that copies of the Bill may be distributed to Members, and the Stationery Office can sell copies to members of the public.

What does our Bill look like? It has a *short title*—"Shops (Hours of Opening) Bill"—and a *long title*, which is "A Bill to regulate the hours of opening of shops; and for other purposes connected therewith." There used to be a *Preamble* to Public Bills in the old times, which explained the reasons for the Bill, but this is hardly ever used to-day except in Private Bills. In the case of an important and complicated Bill there is usually an *Explanatory Memorandum* printed with the Bill, which is a strictly factual explanation of what it contains, but is not part of the Bill itself. If the Bill involves any expenditure which needs to be explained, a strictly factual *Financial Memorandum* is issued with it.

---

1 He would in fact be called "Mr. Secretary—"on the Order Paper.

After the long title on the front page of our Bill there comes the *enacting formula*, which is in the following form:

Be it enacted, by the Queen's Most Excellent Majesty, by and with the advice and consent of the Lords Spiritual and Temporal, and Commons, in this present Parliament assembled, and by the authority of the same, as follows:

If the Bill is one for voting money from the Consolidated Fund or for imposing taxes, the formula begins, "Most Gracious Sovereign, We, Your Majesty's most dutiful and loyal subjects, the Commons of the United Kingdom . . . have resolved . . . etc." To assert the rights of the Commons in the matters of the public money, every "Most Gracious Sovereign" Bill is presented for the Royal Assent personally by the Speaker.

After the enacting formula come the *clauses* of the Bill, which contain the actual proposals, and at the end there may be some *schedules* which give further details, often in the form of a Table. Our Bill reads as follows:

A
BILL
TO

Regulate the hours of opening of shops; and for other purposes connected therewith.

Be it enacted by the Queen's Most Excellent Majesty, by and with the advice and consent of the Lords Spiritual and Temporal, and Commons, in this present Parliament assembled, and by the authority of the same, as follows:

Then come the numbered Clauses, the last one of which reads as follows:

"This Act may be cited as the Shops (Hours of Opening) Act, 196–."

The remark of the Whip that the Bill will be read a second time "To-morrow" does not mean that the Bill will literally be read a second time on the next day, but that it will go down on the list of Bills awaiting the attention of the House.

In the time which elapses between the formal first reading and the second reading, public interest in the Bill will increase considerably. Opposition Members will warn their constituents of the iniquitous nature of the Bill; the Press, the radio, and television will inform a very large audience of the advantages and disadvantages of the proposals, Members will start receiving correspondence on the subject, and interested parties—shop-workers' trade unions, employers, shop-owners and the rest—will attempt to mobilise support for or against the Bill.

On the Thursday before the week in which the Bill is to be read a second time the Leader of the House announces the fact to the House after Question Time. This interlude is one of the most interesting and amusing in the weekly work of the House. The Leader of the Opposition rises and says, "May I ask the Leader of the House if he will announce the business for next week?" The Leader replies, "Yes, sir. The business for next week will be as follows. *Monday, 17th November;* Debate on Foreign Affairs, on the motion for the Adjournment of the House. *Tuesday, 18th November;* Second Reading of the Shops (Hours of Opening) Bill. *Wednesday, 19th November;* Committee and remaining stages of the Civil Airports Bill, which it is hoped to obtain by seven o'clock. There will then be a debate on the Fourth Report from the Committee of Privileges. *Thursday, 20th November;* Second Reading of the Labour Relations (Amendment) Bill, Report and Third Reading of the Aliens (Extradition) Bill *[Lords']*, and discussion of the Agriculture (Tractors and Silage) Order. *Friday, 21st November;* Private Members' Motions."

After the Leader of the Opposition has asked any questions he wishes to raise, back-benchers from both sides leap to their feet to ask the Leader if he is considering giving a debate on a particular subject in which they are individually interested. There is usually some adroit fencing between the Leader and Members which always interests the House.

MR. CHARLES BROWNE: Has my Right Hon. Friend seen a Motion on the Order Paper signed by myself and forty of my Hon. Friends on the subject of a United Nations Police Force, and can he find time for discussion of this very important matter?

THE LEADER OF THE HOUSE: I have noted the Motion of my Hon. Friend, and the Government are very much aware of the extreme importance of the question. I regret that I am unable to give a firm undertaking that we can find time to debate it in the near future, but we shall keep the matter in mind.

MR. JENKS: May I draw the attention of the Leader of the House to the fact that there are many Hon. Members who are extremely interested in the Shops (Hours of Opening) Bill, and particularly in view of the fact that some supporters of the Government are reported in to-day's *Daily Clarion* to be opposed to this stupid and unnecessary Bill, will he suspend the Ten o'clock Rule on Tuesday for an hour so that all these points of view can be raised in the House?

THE LEADER OF THE HOUSE: No, Sir. There is no intention of the Government to stifle discussion on this excellent and far-sighted Bill *(Ministerial cheers and Opposition laughter)*, but it is felt that the usual time will be adequate for all points of view to be expressed.

THE LEADER OF THE OPPOSITION: Yes, but would the Leader of the House care to comment on the report in this day's *Daily Clarion* to which my Hon. Friend referred, to the effect that several Hon. Members opposite are opposed to this ridiculous Bill, and will he arrange for a Free Vote[1] of the House on this important issue?

THE LEADER OF THE HOUSE: No, sir. This is a Government Bill, supported enthusiastically by my Hon. Friends—

---

1 A Free Vote occurs when the Party Whips give no instructions to Members of their party, who may vote as they wish on the subject under discussion

(*Interruption*)—oh, yes, it is. (AN HON. MEMBER: Then why not have a Free Vote and find out?) Because this is a Government measure, and the Government are entitled to put the Whips on to ensure its passage through Parliament . . .

It is to be regretted that much of this fictitious (but not untypical) exchange was political "shadow-boxing." The Opposition would have been greatly astonished if the Government had allowed a Free Vote on such an important Bill, but they can now say that the Government is so unhappy about its own Bill that it is obliged to "put the Whips on" and force it through the House.

SECOND READING

On the day of the Second Reading the Minister and his Undersecretary—who are to make the two speeches at the beginning and end of the debate—have their final discussions in the morning, and polish up their speeches. At the end of Questions they appear in the House behind the Speaker's Chair and take their places on the Treasury Bench. The departmental Civil Servants and the Draftsman wait in the corridor behind the Chair, ready to go into the officials' box when the debate begins.

After Questions and any statements there may be, the Speaker declares, "The Clerk will now proceed to read the Orders of the Day," and the Clerk reads out, "Shops (Hours of Opening) Bill, Second Reading." The Minister rises, hoping that his breezily confident appearance conceals his inward terror, advances to the Dispatch Box, says, "I beg to move that the Bill be read a second time," and embarks upon his prepared speech. At the end of his speech the Speaker *proposes* the Question in these terms: "The Question is, That the Bill be now read a second time." *Debate* now begins, and the Opposition spokesman rises to denounce the Bill, and probably the speech of the Minister as well. Often on these occasions the Opposition moves an Amendment to the Question, giving reasons for rejecting the Bill or else delaying the Second

Reading until "this day six (or, if moved after Whitsun, three) months," If carried, either of these Amendments would kill the Bill.

On Second Reading the *principle* of the Bill is discussed, and debate can range fairly wide. The debate continues until ten o'clock, but in fact the back-benchers are out of it after nine o'clock, when an Opposition front-bencher winds up from his side for thirty minutes or so, and the Minister replies for the Government. At ten o'clock the Question is *put* by the Speaker: "The Question is, That the Bill be now read a second time. As many as are of that opinion say 'Aye' "—"Aye!" roar the Government supporters—"of the contrary 'No' "—"No!" thunderously from the Opposition—"I think the 'Ayes' have it"—"No!" again from the Opposition. "Clear the Lobby!" says the Speaker, and the House proceeds to a Division. Members move towards the two Division Lobbies, one for the Ayes and the other for the Noes, which extend for the full length of the Chamber on either side. Electric division bells are rung all over the building to summon Members to the Chamber, and they have six minutes in which to reach the Lobbies. The Members voting for the Noes go out of the Chamber through the door facing the Speaker behind the Bar, and turn left into the No Lobby; the Ayes go out by the door behind the Chair and turn left into the Aye Lobby. In addition, there are doors at the side of the Chamber which lead directly into the Lobbies.

Two minutes after the Question has been put for the first time the Speaker again puts the Question, and, if his view that the "Ayes" have it is again challenged, he declares, "The Ayes to the right, the Noes to the left. Tellers for the Ayes, Mr. Smith and Mr. Brown, Tellers for the Noes, Mr. Jones and Mr. Robinson." The names of these "Tellers" have been supplied by the appropriate parties, and failure to do so means that the division is "off" and the motion is carried without a division. The Tellers, one from each side, proceed to the exit doors of the Lobbies, which have been locked until now.

Members are probably still arriving at the Chamber, and find a Party Whip standing by the appropriate door, to make sure that none of his flock stray into the wrong Lobby. The Member joins the queue which divides into two streams, one for those whose surnames are in the "A to K" group and the other for those in "L to Z." At the end of the Lobby two Clerks, sitting at high desks, tick off the names of the Members who pass them,[1] before going out through the door and bowing to the Tellers, who are loudly calling out the numbers.

Four minutes after he has appointed the Tellers the Speaker orders, "Lock the doors!" and all entrance doors to the Lobbies are slammed shut by attendants. As soon as all the Members in the Lobbies have voted, the Tellers go to the Table and inform a Clerk at the Table of their numbers. The Clerk writes these down on a slip of paper which he hands to the senior Teller on the winning side; in the case of a division on a Free Vote or when the numbers of Government and Opposition—as in 1950–1, when the Labour majority was eight—are close, this action is viewed with intense interest by the House.

The four Tellers line up before the Mace, those for the winning side on the Speaker's left. The Speaker calls "Order! Order!" The Tellers bow, advance one step, bow again, and the winning Teller reads out the figures. The piece of paper is handed to a Clerk, who is standing beside the Opposition dispatch box, and he takes it to the Speaker, who reads the figures out again, adding, "So the Ayes (or the Noes) have it." The Tellers return to their places, the Serjeant at Arms orders the doors to the division Lobbies to be unlocked, and the House proceeds to its next business. The whole process of taking a division when there are over four hundred members present takes about ten to fifteen minutes.

Assuming that the Government obtains its usual majority, the Bill is declared to be read a second time, and committed to a Standing Committee, unless a motion is carried to commit it to a Committee of the Whole House.

What happens next? First of all, the Speaker decides—usually after consultation with the Government and the Public Bill Office—

---

1 The names are published in *Hansard* and in a supplement to the *Votes and Proceedings*. Publication of division lists has been done since 1836, and is useful for the Whips and the public to see how individual Members have voted.

to which Standing Committee (A, B, D, etc.[1]) the Bill should be referred, and formally allocates the Bill. This fact is recorded as a memorandum to the *Votes and Proceedings*. He then appoints a Chairman from the Chairmen's Panel to preside over the Committee, whose members are chosen by the Committee of Selection (see Chapter Eight). When the names of the members of the Committee have been published, the Bill is ready for discussion.

THE BILL IN COMMITTEE

On Second Reading the *principle* of the Bill was discussed; in Committee the *details* of the Bill are examined Clause by Clause. There can be no discussion on Clause Two so long as someone wants to speak on Clause One (unless the Government move the Closure) and there is no limit on the number of times Members can speak.

The atmosphere of a Standing Committee is usually friendly and courteous. Amendments which may be sent in by any Member but which can only be moved by those who are on the Committee, are sent to the Public Bill Office, where they are checked. This checking is purely to make sure that the amendments refer to the correct page and line in the Bill, and if there has been an error, it is corrected, and the Amendment put into the correct form. It is then sent to the printer, and a list appears on each day of the Amendments which have been put down. A few days before the Committee meets for the first time, these Amendments are "marshalled" into a list in which they are put in the correct order.

A senior Clerk in the Public Bill Office is responsible for the Bill's Committee Stage from the Parliamentary point of view, and he advises the Chairman on procedural matters both in the Committee and in conferences, when they go through the Bill and the Amendments together. The Draftsman is also available for consultation. The Chairman chooses the date of the first meeting

---

1 Standing Committee C is usually reserved for Private Members' Bills. Bills relating exclusively to Scotland are referred to the Scottish Standing Committee.

and notices are sent to each member of the Committee informing him of this fact. When the Committee meets for the first time the Amendment Sheet might read as follows:

SHOPS (HOURS OF OPENING) BILL

Mr. Thompson

Mr. Sharp

Clause 1, page 1, line 5, after "if" insert "the Minister, on application from a local authority or".

Mr. Greig

Mrs. Trend

Clause 1, page 1, line 7, leave out "shall instruct the appropriate" and insert, "shall, after consultation with the appropriate local authority, request it".

Mr. Secretary—(The Home Secretary)

Clause 1, page 1, line 9, leave out "shall" and insert "may"...

A Standing Committee is the House in miniature. It meets in one of the large Committee Rooms on the Committee Corridor, and the Members sit on either side of the Chairman, facing each other, as in the House. The Chairman sits on a raised platform, on which are grouped other officials. To his right there is the Draftsman and the departmental Civil Servants, who advise the Minister; on his left there are the senior and junior Clerks from the Public Bill Office and the senior *Hansard* reporter, who is responsible for the management of the Official Report of the Committee. The Members sit on chairs behind long desks, more Government and opposition facing one another as in the House. Between the "front benches" there is a small table for the *Hansard* reporters, and at the end of the room there are benches for spectators.

Before the Committee can examine the Amendments which have been tabled, it must decide when it is going to meet in future. The Minister in charge of the Bill moves a "sittings motion," which is usually in the form, "That the Committee do meet on Tuesdays and Thursdays at half past ten o'clock." Normally this motion is accepted without discussion, but in the case of a controversial Bill, the Opposition will probably challenge the motion, and even move Amendments to shorten the hours of meeting or change the days. Discussion on this can rage happily all morning, and be concluded by the Government moving the Closure just before one o'clock. In the event of a Division, the junior Clerk reads out the names of members of the Committee, and each will call out "Aye" or "No" as the case may be. The result is then announced to the Committee by the Chairman.

When the Committee has decided when it is to meet, the Bill itself can be examined. Mr. Thompson rises to move his Amendment in page 1, line 5, after the word "if," to insert the words "the Minister, on application from a local authority or." Behind this dry formula we discover that there lie mighty principles. If the Amendment is accepted, and the words written into the Bill, it means that unless a local authority applies to the Minister for permission to enforce the provisions of the Bill in its area, then the Bill would not apply in that locality. Mr. Thompson moves his harmless-looking Amendment, arguing that local authorities should have the right to decide what hours the shops in its area should remain open; the Minister replies that the Amendment would destroy the whole purpose of the Bill and must be rejected; other Members join in the debate, which will inevitably result in the defeat of the Amendment, unless the Government Whips are asleep or several of the Government supporters feel so strongly that they either vote against the Minister or abstain. Then Mr. Greig rises to move his Amendment (page 1, line 7, leave out "shall instruct the appropriate" and insert "shall, after consultation with the appropriate local authority, request it") and explains the reasons which prompted him to suggest this improvement in the Bill. Perhaps it is a genuine suggestion, or it may be another Opposition attempt to make the Bill useless; the Minister and his advisers will have made up their minds on this before now, and he will reply accordingly. After all the Amendments to a Clause have been dealt with, the Committee can then debate, and, if they desire, divide on, the Question that "the Clause (as amended) stand part of the Bill."

And so our Bill moves on, from ten-thirty to one o'clock (when the Committee automatically adjourns "without Question put, pursuant to the Standing Order") on Tuesday and Thursday mornings. Whenever an Amendment is made to the Bill, the senior Clerk records the alteration in a special copy of the Bill. The junior Clerk keeps the Minutes of the Committee—like the Journals and the *Votes and Proceedings*, these record only *decisions* of the Committee and only set out those Amendments which are rejected on the grounds that if Amendments are made they will form part of the amended Bill reported to the House—while a succession of *Hansard* reporters take down the verbatim speeches. The Chairman, advised by the senior Clerk on matters of procedure, and by the Draftsman on legal questions, controls the proceedings of the Committee. He can rule Amendments out of order for various technical reasons, and he can simply not select others for discussion. He exercises the latter power when he considers that adequate notice has not been given of the Amendment,[1] or if he thinks it is unnecessary. He can also suggest to the Committee that they discuss a series of Amendments which cover the same point together on one particular Amendment, to expedite the work of the Committee. His powers are not as great as those of the Speaker or the Chairman of Ways and Means in matters of discipline—he cannot, for example, suspend a Member—but his rulings are based upon the procedure of the House, and he is usually given support by the Committee.

If the proceedings on the Bill are going on far too long for the liking of the Government, the hours of meeting can be extended, so that the Committee can meet on three mornings a week and even on some evenings. This will be strenuously opposed by the Opposition, and if the extra time does not lead to greater speed, the Government may have to employ what is known as the "Guillotine." This is an Order of the House which states that the Bill must finish its Committee Stage on such-and-such a date. A business sub-committee, consisting of Members from both sides of the Committee, will then meet to draw up a time-table. This "time-

---

1 Those Amendments which were put down only the day before the Committee meets are marked with a "star" and "starred" Amendments are very rarely selected for discussion.

table" is simply that Clause X shall be finished on the Tuesday, Clause Y on the Wednesday, and so on. At the time laid down, the Chairman has to bring discussion to an end and put the Question forthwith "That the Clause (as amended) stand part of the Bill." This procedure is invariably opposed by the Opposition, and cries of "Gag!" are hurled at the Government.

But it is not often that the Government has to turn to such measures, and the work of a Standing Committee, although often dull, is normally conducted in a co-operative atmosphere. When all the Clauses and the Schedules of the Bill have been approved, any new Clauses debated, rejected or added, the Chairman is ordered to report the Bill (as amended) to the House. This is done formally by the Clerk, and the House orders the amended Bill to be reprinted; the Public Bill Office and the Draftsman, having checked that all the Amendments are incorporated, arrange for the new Bill to be published, and it is now ready for its next stage.

REPORT STAGE

The Report—or "consideration"—Stage is for the purpose of enabling the House to see what its Standing Committee has done to the Bill, and to give further opportunity for amendment.[1] The difference between Committee Stage and Report Stage is that in the latter the Speaker is in the Chair, Members may not speak twice on the same Question without the leave of the House, and only Amendments which have been put down are discussed. There is no discussion of "Clause stand part"; if there are no amendments to Clause 1, then that Clause will not be discussed at all. The Clerk of the House advises the Speaker on the Amendments tabled, and as a general rule, Amendments which have been exhaustively discussed in Committee are not selected on Report. Report Stage gives an opportunity for Ministers to move new Amendments to fulfil undertakings they gave in Committee or to cover loopholes which were discovered by discussions in the course of the progress

1 There is no Report Stage if the Bill returns unamended from a Committee of the Whole House.

of the Bill, and the Opposition may renew its attacks on certain aspects of it.

THIRD READING

This is the last stage in the Commons. On Second Reading the principle of our Bill was discussed; in Committee it was examined in detail; Report Stage gave the House an opportunity of further amending the details, and, if necessary, of overriding the decisions of its Committee. On Third Reading the *completed* Bill is discussed, and the debate is very restricted, although the House can, even at this late stage, reject the Bill on a division. With the exception of the most fiercely contested measures, the Third Reading debate is comparatively brief and friendly. When the motion has been passed the Bill is reprinted under the inspection of the Public Bill Office and finally checked, and the "Act Copy"—the word "Bill" having now been dropped—is sent to the House of Lords. The Public Bill Office informs the Clerk of the House of the time the Lords are sitting, and prepares a message to the Lords. In this case it will simply read:

The Commons have passed—

The Shops (Hours of Opening) Bill,

to which they desire the agreement of the Lords.

The Clerk writes on the first page of the Act Copy "*Soit baillé aux Seigneurs*," signs his name at the end of the Bill, and, carrying the Bill and the Message tied together with green ribbon, takes it personally to the Bar of the House of Lords, where it is received by the Clerk of the Parliaments or one of the other Lords' Clerks.

If the Lords agree to the Bill, they merely send a message announcing the fact, and the Bill is ready for the Royal Assent. But if they make Amendments, the "Act Copy" is returned with details of these Amendments, together with a message requesting the agreement of the Commons. The Government will have to find time for consideration of these Amendments, and when this arrives the Minister moves "That the Lords' Amendments be now considered," and, upon this being agreed to, the Amendments are considered one by one. If they are all agreed to, a message announcing this fact is communicated in a message to the Lords, again borne down the corridors, and across the lobbies by the gowned and wigged Clerk. At one time there used to be some ceremony about this to-ing and fro-ing and when the Home Rule Bill for Ireland was carried to the Lords in 1893, Liberal Members cheered the Clerk on his way. Nowadays he is obliged to dodge queues of Strangers waiting to see their Members, and politely make his way through the milling crowd in the Central Hall.

If the Commons disagree to any of the Lords' Amendments, they choose a small Committee after all the Amendments have been examined, which meets at once in a small room behind the Speaker's Chair to draw up reasons for the disagreement, and these are conveyed to their Lordships. If the Lords refuse to accept the Commons' disagreements the Bill comes winging back down the corridors and the Commons have to reconsider the matter; in the case of complete deadlock the Bill will probably be killed for lack of time, as all Bills—with the exception of certain Private Bills—which have not received the Royal Assent by the end of the Session disappear, and must begin the weary round again in the new Session if they are to become law. But a complete disagreement between the two Houses is very rare indeed; if the Commons stick their toes in and refuse to accept any of the Lords' Amendments, the Lords will almost certainly give way.

Our Bill, now in a very different condition from when it started, is ready for the Royal Assent. This is signified by a Royal Commission which meets in the House of Lords—the Assent has not been given in person by the Monarch since 1854—and when the Speaker, the Clerk, and Members of the Commons, summoned by Black Rod, are assembled at the Bar, the Clerk of the Crown reads out the title of the Bill, and the Clerk of the Parliaments says "*La Reyne le veult,*" which is Norman French for "The Queen so wills it." In the case of a Bill for granting money the formula is *"La Reyne remercie ses bons sujets, accepte leur benevolence, et ainsi le veult"*—"The Queen thanks her kind subjects, accepts their grant, and also wills it"(or, less literally, "approves the Bill"). The "Act Copy," by now somewhat battered and heavily covered with the Anglo-Norman messages written by the Clerk of the House and the Clerk of the Parliaments, is preserved in the House of Lords.

Our Bill is now an Act of Parliament, enshrined in the "Statute Book" as part of the law of the land and can now only be repealed by another Act of Parliament.

PRIVATE MEMBERS' BILLS

Government business has precedence at all except a small number of sittings of the House, and these are known as "Private Members' Days." The days set aside for back-bench Members are divided into "Bill days" and "Motions days," and, as there are always more Members who want to introduce Bills and move motions than there is time, they ballot for the chance of introducing a Bill or Motion.

In the case of Bills, the ballot is held early in the Session. For two sitting days early in November, Members can go to one of the Clerks from the Public Bill Office, who is sitting in the "No" Lobby, and put their names down against a number in a large book. The Chairman of Ways and Means, assisted by the Clerks, actually conducts the business of the ballot on a following morning in a Committee Room, when he picks out folded slips of paper, each with a number on it, from a large black dispatch box. The first twenty Members out of the ballot may introduce a Bill, but in effect only the first six have much chance of getting anywhere— unless the others are very uncontroversial—since there are only six "Bill days" set aside for Second Readings. The first six successful candidates in the ballot usually choose these days, and their successors put down their Bills after them. Some careful calculation is needed at this point, since it may be that one or other of the successful six has a tiny uncontroversial Bill which should occupy no time at all, so there is some competition in the "second string" to get their Bills down for the same day. The Members are responsible for drafting and presenting their own Bills, although the Government may help to draft a Bill of which they approve, and usually one or two Private Members' Bills are trivial Government Bills, actually drafted by Departments and pressed fondly upon a Member who has no ideas about what Bill he is to introduce.

In any event, although the Member may have no chance of getting his Bill through, particularly if he is a member of the Opposition and the Government dislike his Bill, the mere fact that it has been published may pave the way for success at a later stage. The Merchant Shipping Act of the 1870's, which obliged ships to have a loading line—"the Plimsoll line"—around the hull to prevent overloading, started life as a Private Member's Bill introduced by Mr. Plimsoll. The law of divorce was considerably altered by a Private Member's Bill piloted through the Commons by Sir Alan Herbert in 1937.

Private Members' days can be great fun, and are excellent training-grounds for aspiring Parliamentarians. It may be that Bill A is an utterly harmless little Bill blessed by the Government, but Bill B is very controversial, and opposed by the Government. To the surprise of some people, the debate on Bill A will go on for a long time, to the fury of the supporters of Bill B. The discussion on Private Member's Bills must end at four o'clock on a Friday, and the Chair would only allow the Closure for a Bill which has been discussed for almost all the day. If Bill A is agreed to at three o'clock, there is only an hour for Bill B, and at four o'clock an opponent of the Bill will be still on his feet; if there is an attempt to move the Closure, the Chair will certainly refuse to accept it, so the Bill is "talked out," and must come up again on a later Friday, when its chances of getting a Second Reading are negligible. There are other stratagems which can be artfully employed, such as drawing attention to the absence of a quorum with the hope of "counting the House out", which temporarily kills the Bill under discussion and also kills the other Bills down for the same day. It is not unknown for opponents of Bill C to concentrate their fire on Bill B—about which there may be no interest—and, by holding up that Bill, destroy the chances of the other.

Members can also introduce Bills under what is popularly known as the "Ten-Minute Rule." These are motions asking for leave to bring in a Bill, and the procedure enables a Member to make a brief speech in support of his measure. This motion can only be moved on a Tuesday or Wednesday, and takes place before the main business of the day after Questions. Another Member may oppose the motion, and then the Question "That leave be given to bring in the Bill" is put by the Speaker. If it is agreed to, the Member is asked, "Who will prepare and bring in this Bill?" to which the Member replies by reading out the names of his supporters, ending with the modest, "and myself, Sir." He then goes to the Bar of the House, and, on being called by the Speaker, advances up the Floor, bowing to the Chair, and hands his "dummy" Bill (see page 85) to the Clerk, who reads out the title. "Second Reading, what day?" inquires Mr. Speaker, and the Member replies, "Friday next, sir," or whatever the day which he has chosen may be. The Bill then goes to the bottom of the list of Bills down for discussion that day, and often this is the last that the House will hear of it. Whenever it comes up at four o'clock on the Friday— when all the outstanding Bills are read out by the Clerk—it only needs one Member to cry, "Object!" and it will be put off for another week.

Although the chances of a Private Member's Bill actually becoming law are small unless the Government supports it, it gives Private Members an excellent opportunity of drawing attention to anomalies in the law, illogicalities, or even injustices, and, for the Opposition, of making the Government "show its hand" on a particular matter. A Bill introduced by an Opposition Member in the Session 1955–6 which made factories liable for rates in the same way as private houses, and which was opposed by the Government, received a Second Reading as a result of some intensive secret "whipping" by the promoter, and it even passed unamended through a Standing Committee. This was achieved by a carefully planned and well-executed manœuvre. On the first day on which the Committee sat, a succession of Opposition Members spoke at great length on "Clause One stand part"—this being the only important Clause in the Bill?—and the Committee was obliged to meet again on the next sitting day. When the Committee assembled, the Government had an adequate majority, and one or two Government supporters who had other engagements were allowed to leave the Committee in view of this fact. To the surprise of the Government, the debate collapsed almost at once, and a division was called. Through the doors poured a sudden influx of Opposition Members, and the motion was carried against the Government. It later transpired that the Opposition Members had arrived early, and had concealed themselves in a nearby Committee Room until the Division was called. The Bill returned to the House and after a three-line Whip had been issued by the Government it was defeated on Third Reading, although not before the Government had suffered a certain amount of embarrassing ridicule and attack. This is one example of how the procedure for Private Members' Bills can be used by an ingenious Member to humiliate the Government, and there have been occasions—as in the case of Mr. Sydney Silverman's Bill to abolish the death penalty in 1956, which was defeated eventually in the Lords—when the Government has been forced to introduce legislation of its own as a result of pressure aroused by a Private Member's Bill.

PRIVATE BILLS

We now move on to the third category of Bills, Private Bills. These have an entirely different procedure to Public Bills, and have their own Standing Orders. The field of private legislation is extremely complicated, so we will follow the course of another imaginary (but not untypical) Bill.

Oxbridge Borough Council desires to promote a Private Bill to enable it compulsorily to acquire property, introduce new by-laws, and for other local purposes. Having passed a Resolution to this effect, the Council instructs the Town Clerk to proceed to draw up the Bill. He contacts one of several firms of solicitors who are "Parliamentary Agents," and who are permitted by Mr. Speaker to present Bills to Parliament. These firms take on the task of the Parliamentary Draftsman in the case of a Public Bill, and their Draft Bill must be approved by the Council. Due notice, in the *London Gazette* and local papers, must be given of the Bill, so that any interested local citizen may see what it proposes. If over a hundred express strong disapproval, a "Town Poll" is held, at which the opponents of the Bill—perhaps those who are going to have their property taken away by the compulsory powers, or who are opposed to an increase in the rates which the Bill may involve— try to carry a motion hostile to the Bill which, if passed, settles the matter there and then. We will assume that Oxbridge Borough Council win the day, and their Bill goes forward.

A petition, praying that leave may be given to bring in the Bill, together with a copy of the Bill itself, is presented to the Private Bill Office before the end of November. It then goes to one of the *Examiners*, who are two senior Clerks from the Lords and Commons, and who summon the Promoters before them to see that all the Standing Orders have been complied with. They will particularly inquire whether the notices in the newspapers were properly inserted and that all individuals affected by the Bill have been warned. If the Standing Orders have been complied with, the Examiners report accordingly to the House, and the Bill proceeds. If they have been transgressed, another body, the *Standing Orders Committee*, looks into the matter and makes a Report to the House. The Chairman of Ways and Means and the Chairman of Committees in the Lords have, in the meanwhile, decided which Bills are to start in the Lords, and which in the Commons.

Any person or group of persons affected by the Bill may petition against it, and these petitions must be presented in a certain form by the end of January. Usually they are drafted by firms of Agents, but private citizens sometimes prepare their own and are advised by the Clerks in the Private Bill Office. All Bills thus petitioned against are "opposed" Bills, and those without *contra*-petitions are "unopposed Bills." They all come up for First Reading—which is purely formal—on a day specified by the Standing Orders in February.

Now, let us suppose that a certain citizen of Oxbridge is personally affected by the Oxbridge Bill, in that some property opposite his house is going to be compulsorily acquired by the Council if the Bill passes. The Corporation intend to build a gas-works on the land, so that the value of his house will be severely affected. He lodges a Petition against the Bill through one of the Agents, and decides to engage a barrister to argue his case. He also writes to his Member, asking him to assist him. The Member for Oxbridge may well be reluctant to oppose a Bill proposed by his local authority—most Members are—but agrees that his constituent has a case, and should receive better compensation for the loss of the value of his property. If the Promoters refuse to agree, the Member will "block" the Bill in the House.

Private Business is the first item on the Commons' agenda after Prayers, and the Bills are printed on the first page of the Order Paper. The Speaker says, "The Clerk will now proceed to read the titles of Private Bills set down for consideration this day," and the Clerk begins to read out the titles. If there is no objection, the Bills are declared to have passed that stage of their progress; if objection is taken the Bill is put down by the Chairman of Ways and Means for another day. When the Clerk reads out "Second Reading Oxbridge Corporation Bill" the Member for Oxbridge calls out "Object!", the Speaker says, "Second reading, what day?" the Chairman of Ways and Means, who has a general responsibility for Private Bills, names a day, and the House moves on to consider the next Bill on the list.

The Town Clerk of Oxbridge, sitting under the Gallery behind the chair of the Serjeant at Arms, is not pleased, nor are the Parliamentary Agents. Fees are charged by the House for every stage of a Bill, and one Member shouting "Object!" can at once add £1 to the bill. The Member is button-holed in the Lobby;

would he be so good as to explain why he objected to the Bill? He explains, and asks if something can be done for people like his constituent. The answer is that no undertaking can be given; the Member replies that in that event he must go on objecting to the Bill.

After a few days of the unfortunate Bill coming up and the Member for Oxbridge shouting "Object!" the Chairman of Ways and Means orders the Bill to be put down for such-and-such a day at seven o'clock in the evening. The Member for Oxbridge has at least secured a debate for his constituent, and the Promoters of the Bill hurriedly look around for a Member to support the Bill in the debate.

It is rare for a Private Bill to be defeated on Second Reading, as the House tends to take the view that it does not know enough about the details of the case, and refers these problems to a Private Bill Committee.

Meanwhile, the Petition is getting into trouble. The Promotors have lodged an objection to it, on the grounds that the Petitioner is merely a ratepayer, and that he has no right—or *locus standi*, to use the proper phrase—to have his Petition heard by a Committee of the House. What rights he had, the Promoters argue, went when the Town Poll supported the Bill.

These arguments, and those for the Petitioner, are brought before the *Court of Referees*, a Committee of the House of which the Chairman is the Chairman of Ways and Means, and whose Members are assisted by Mr. Speaker's Counsel.[1] Barristers appear before this Court for the Promoters and the Petitioner, and the Court has to decide whether the Petitioner—who is probably beginning to think that he is going to lose more money by lawyers' fees than he would if the gas-works were built and the value of his house destroyed—can appear before the Private Bill Committee. They decide that as he is directly and personally affected by parts of the Bill he can have a *locus* against those Clauses which affect him.

---

1 This title is rather misleading, for he is rarely called upon to advise the Speaker. He is an experienced lawyer who is an Officer of the House, assists the Chairman of Ways and Means in his examination of Private Bills, and sits on various Committees such as the Court of Referees.

The first hurdle—and one which brings down many private Petitioners—has been safely surmounted.

The Private Bill Committee to consider the Oxbridge Corporation Bill is chosen by the Committee of Selection (see pages 131–2), who also appoint the Chairman and set the date for the Committee's first meeting. The Committee will consist of four Members, two from each side of the House, who must not have any connection with the area concerned, nor have demonstrated any views on the subject; in direct contrast with Public Bills, any Member who spoke or voted on Second Reading is debarred from membership of the Committee. (If the Bill had not been opposed, in that there were no petitions against it, or they had all been withdrawn, a Committee on Unopposed Bills, chosen by the Chairman of Ways and Means from a special Panel of Members set up at the beginning of the Session by the Committee of Selection, would have considered the Bill.)

In a Private Bill Committee the Members are really in the position of Judges in a Court of Law. Barristers argue the cases before them, and witnesses are sworn and cross-examined. The Committee has to make up its mind first and foremost if the principle of the Bill is acceptable. This is known as "Proving the Preamble." If the Preamble is not proved, then the Bill is finished; if it is proved, the Committee goes on to examine the Clauses of the Bill, and can examine the Promoters.

Counsel for the Oxbridge Bill opens up, and occupies the best part of the first day (Committees usually meet from eleven to one, and two to four o'clock) with his opening speech. He reads out the Petitions and any observations which Government Departments may have put in. He then calls witnesses, examines them, and counsel for the Petitioners cross-examines them.

When the Promoters' counsel has finished, counsel for the Petitioners addresses the Committee, and calls witnesses, who can be cross-examined by the Promoters' counsel. As each counsel comes to important points in his case he may hand in papers to the Committee—copies of letters or other documents, maps, or even photographs—to assist his argument.

The Petitioner is called as a witness, and his counsel asks him questions about which he has had warning, and in which he has perhaps been rehearsed; the Promoters' counsel then cross-examines him, attempting to throw doubts upon his complaints, and after he has finished the Petitioner's counsel may re-examine him for a few minutes to clear up any possible misunderstandings. Then the Committee ask a few questions, and the Petitioner's ordeal is over. After they have heard all the evidence and final speeches from the two counsels, the Chairman orders the room to be cleared, and the Committee deliberate in private.

They decide that the Bill as a whole should be passed, but that there should be greater compensation to people like the Petitioner whose property will be affected by the Bill.[1] The parties are recalled by the Clerk to the Committee, and when they are all present the Chairman informs them that "The Committee find the Preamble proved (an audible sigh of relief from the Oxbridge Town Clerk), *but* (a grim look comes over his face) they instruct the Promoters to insert into the Bill more generous provision for property-owners who will be dispossessed by Part I of the Bill. These provisions should follow these lines . . ."

When the Promoters have amended those parts of the Bill which are objected to, they submit them to the Petitioners, and if they are still not satisfied, the Committee will have to judge on the matter. If everyone is agreeable to the new provisions, the Committee pass the relevant Clauses and the Chairman signs the Bill, which is reprinted (as amended) by the Promoters.

The remaining stages of the Bill—consideration and Third Reading—are the same as for a Public Bill, except that if a single Member still objects when the Bill comes up at the time of Private Business after Prayers, it is postponed until time can be found for a seven o'clock debate. This does not happen often, but if the Petitioner was not satisfied and could persuade his Member, that Member could put down Amendments on consideration and even if they were not carried, he could delay the progress of the Bill so

---

1 In the event of a division the Chairman may vote, and if the numbers are equal, he has a casting vote.

much that the Promoters might decide to cut their losses and give way.

Many arguments—which usually come from Promoters—can be raised against the Private Bill procedure. It is lengthy, complicated, extremely expensive, and uncertain. Private Bill Committee-members are seldom lawyers, and their judgments can sometimes be curious law, although they are usually good justice. But, on the whole, this assists the Petitioner, which is as it should be, for he is spending his time and money defending what he has; the Promoters are going to get something out of the Bill, so they should have to make their case to the satisfaction of the Committee. But perhaps the greatest objections to the procedure are its complexity and expense. Petitioners must have money if they are going to engage lawyers, and if the individual decides to fight the case himself—assuming that he can spare the time—be is liable to be outwitted by the trained barrister. Most Petitions are lodged by local authorities or other large undertakings, who can afford this costly and prolonged procedure, and it is a truism of all good law that it must be simple for the laymen to understand and easy for him to protect his interests. At the present it is arguable that the odds are weighed too heavily in favour of the Promoters and wealthy Petitioners, and this is not a healthy situation, even though it is mitigated by the fairness of Private Bill Committees.

And so we come to the end of this account of how various kinds of Acts of Parliament are passed. The complexities of the procedure are so great that it is difficult to present a simple portrait of how the machinery works, but it will have been seen that it is designed to ensure that little can become law which has not been thoroughly discussed by both Houses, by a system of "checks and balances," assisted by the pressure of public opinion, to prevent stupid and unworkable Acts of Parliament. And the very length of time between the introduction of the average Bill and the receiving of the Royal Assent is, in itself, a safeguard of the rights of the individual. It is when legislation is rushed through with too little thought and no careful scrutiny that injustice occurs.

CHAPTER SEVEN

The Records of the House

Early in the morning of 23rd March, 1831, the House of Commons proceeded to a Division on the Second Reading of the First Reform Bill. This Bill, which was designed to alter the representation laws of the country, so that many more people could vote in elections and that many constituencies could become more representative, had aroused the most violent feelings in the country. In retrospect, it appears a mild enough measure whose effects were not very great, but to contemporaries it appeared to be a tremendous step forward, and the beginning of the end of the domination of the upper classes. The historian, Macaulay, was a Member of Parliament, and he has penned an unforgettable account of the conclusion of the tense and exciting debate which had lasted for several days.

> ... The crowd overflowed the House in every part. When the Strangers were cleared out[1] and the doors were locked, we had 608 members present—more by 45 than ever were in a division before. The Ayes and the Noes were like two volleys of cannon from opposite sides of a field of battle. When the Opposition went out into the Lobby,[2] an operation which took up twenty minutes or more, we spread ourselves over the benches on both

---

1 At that time, and indeed until about seventy years ago, the galleries were cleared when the House proceeded to a division.
2 In the old House of Commons, the Ayes remained in the House to be counted, and the Noes went into the Lobby

sides of the House; for there were many of us who were not able to find a seat during the evening.

When the doors were shut, we began to speculate on our numbers. Everybody was desponding. "We have lost it. We are only 280 at most. I do not think we are 250. They are 300. Alderman Thompson has counted them. He says they are 299." This was the talk on our benches . . . I had no hope, however, of 300. As the tellers passed along our lowest row on the left-hand side the interest was insupportable—291, 292—we were all standing up and stretching forward, telling with the tellers. At 300 there was a short cry of joy, at 302 another, suppressed, however, in a moment, for we did not know what the hostile force might be. We knew, however, that we should not be severely beaten.

The doors were thrown open, and in they came. Each as he entered brought some different report of their numbers . . . We were all breathless when Charles Wood, who stood near the door, jumped on a bench and cried out, "They are only 301." We set up such a shout that you might have heard to Charing Cross, waving our hats, stamping on the floor, and clapping our hands. The tellers scarcely got through the crowd, for the House was thronged up to the table, and all the floor was fluctuating with heads like the pit of a theatre. But you might have heard a pin drop as Duncannon read the numbers. Then again the shouts broke out, and many of us shed tears. I could scarcely refrain. And the jaw of Peel fell; and the face of Twiss was as the face of a damned soul; and Herries looked like Judas taking his necktie off for the last operation.[1] We shook hands and clapped each other on the back, and went out laughing, crying, and huzzaing into the Lobby. And no sooner were the doors opened than another shout answered that within the House. All the passages and stairs in the waiting-rooms were thronged by people who had waited till four o'clock in the morning to know the issue. We passed through a narrow lane between two thick masses of them; and all the way down they

---

1 Leading opponents of the Bill.

were shouting and waving their hats, till we got into the open air. I called a cabriolet, and the first thing the driver asked was, "Is the Bill carried?" "Yes, by one." "Thank God for that!" And away I rode to Gray's Inn . . .

If one turns to the official record of that momentous division in the *Journals of the House*, one finds the following entry:

Ordered. That the Order of the Day, for resuming the adjourned Debate upon the Amendments which were yesterday proposed to the Motion, That the Bill to amend the Representation of the People in *England* and *Wales*, be now read a second time; and which Amendments were to leave out the word "now," and, at the end of the Question, to add the words "upon this day six months," be now read; and the same being read: The House resumed the said adjourned Debate.

And the Question being again proposed, That the word "now" stand part of the Question:

And the House having continued to sit till after Twelve of the clock on Wednesday morning;

Mercurii, 23° die Martii, 1831;

And the Question being put; That the word "now" stand part of the Question;

The House divided.

The Noes went forth.

| Tellers for the Yeas, | { Lord Viscount *Duncannon*
 Mr. *Spring Rice* } | 302 |
| Tellers for the Noes, | { Marquis of Chandos
 Sir George Clerk } | 301 |

So it was resolved in the Affirmative.

Then the main Question being put:

Ordered, That the Bill be now read a second time:—The Bill was accordingly read a second time; and committed to a Committee of the Whole House for Thursday, the 14th day of April next.

This contrast demonstrates the function of the *Journals of the House*, which are the official records of the House of Commons. They are to record what the House *decides*; with the exception of certain speeches of the Speaker or the Sovereign, no reference is made to speeches, to Question Time, or Ministerial Statements. So far as the Journal is concerned, these do not exist. The Journal records the papers laid on the Table by the Speaker, Reports made to the House by Chairman of Committees, and decisions of the House. The style and language of the seventeenth century are still employed in the Journal, so that although the "Ayes" vote accordingly in the House, the Journal obstinately persists in calling them the "Yeas," and if a motion is defeated, the Journal announces firmly, "So it was resolved in the Negative."

The Journal is prepared in the Clerk's department under the authority of the Speaker, and is published at the end of every Session of Parliament. It is compiled by Clerks in the Journal Office from the Minute Books kept by the Clerks at the Table, which serve as their authority. It is the only authentic and authoritative record of the proceedings of the House, and, if necessary, can be produced in a Court of Law as evidence of what the House has done.

On every morning after the House has sat, the Journal Office publish (again, under the authority of the Speaker) *The Votes and Proceedings of the House of Commons*, which is a shorter and simpler version of the Journal, but which follows much the same rules. No reference whatever is made to Questions, Statements, or speeches; only what the House does is recorded. Thus, some of Sir Winston Churchill's greatest war speeches were made on motions for the Adjournment of the House, and the only reference which the *Vote* makes to the occasion is in the entry "Motion made and Question proposed, That this House do now adjourn—(Mr. Churchill):—Motion, by leave, *withdrawn*."

The *Journals of the House* are of great antiquity, and the public records go back to 1547 (although some subsequent years are missing from the collection). The *Votes and Proceedings* date from

1680, and since 1690 they have been printed daily under the order of the House, which is passed at the beginning of every Session.

The House is sitting; Questions and Statements are over, and the Orders of the Day have been entered upon. The business is the Report Stage of an important Bill. Members move Amendments, which are either withdrawn, accepted, or defeated. There is always one Clerk at the Table who is recording these decisions in his Minute Book. From time to time he is relieved by one of his colleagues at the Table who continues to record the proceedings of the House in his Minute Book. The Minute Book of the Clerk who comes off duty is collected by a messenger, and sent to the Journal Office high above the Chamber: the *Vote* is written in manuscript, and sent to be printed. A "proof" copy is sent back, and after the House has risen, both Minute Books are checked with the proof. One of the Clerks from the Table attends in case there are any questions raised, and the printer is also there. The proof is then given to the printer, who arranges for the corrected *Votes and Proceedings* to be printed during the night and published on the following morning.

HANSARD

On every morning from Tuesday to Saturday while the House of Commons is sitting, there is produced one of the miracles of publication, the "Official Report" of the proceedings in the House, *alias* "Hansard." This small book recounts, with astonishing accuracy, almost every word spoken in the House from the moment that Mr. Speaker calls, "Order, Order," at the commencement of business, until 10.30 p.m. Sir Alan Herbert, himself Independent Member for Oxford University for fifteen years, has written wittily and wisely upon this subject.

Read *Hansard*. For the papers cannot tell
The many things that Parliament does well.
How many a Member labours many days

To find his figures and perfect his phrase,
And waits and waits, while many a meal goes by,
Hungry and worn, to catch the Speaker's Eye,
Pours out his heart, his wisdom and his jokes,
And is enrolled among the "Also Spoke's"!
You'll be surprised, good citizens, to see
How right your representatives can be!
It should be cheaper; sixpence is a shame:
But it's a good sixpenn'orth, all the same.[1]

Hansard now costs a shilling for the daily volume, but Sir Alan's tribute is equally deserved.

In 1803, when the House was relaxing its previously hostile attitude towards the reporting of its debate, William Cobbett published with his *Political Register* a report of the debates in the House, and in 1811 he sold out his interest to his printer, Thomas Curzon Hansard, whose father was the official printer of the *Journals of the House*. For nearly eighty years the firm of Hansard published the report of proceedings in the House, but these were not verbatim reports—in other words, written down at the time by reporters—but were compiled from those which appeared in *The Times* and other leading newspapers and were not published daily. In 1878 a Select Committee of the House recommended that a grant should be paid to the firm out of Stationery Office Funds, and the first *Hansard* reporter was appointed to take down verbatim what was said in the House. For some time, however, the low quality of the reporting had been the subject of complaints by Members, and in 1888 another Select Committee recommended greater control by the Government; the then T. C. Hansard—the son of the original Hansard—refused to continue publication on these terms, and there ensued an unhappy period when a series of firms took over the responsibility, went bankrupt, and disappeared. In 1907 the Government accepted the prevalent opinion that it must take over this important and ill-conducted function. Thus was the "Official Report" born in 1909 and "Hansard" killed. So

---

1 Printed in the *Sunday Graphic*, 19th September, 1948.

deeply did the first editors of the new report despise the old version that the very word "Hansard" was not allowed to appear until 1943, when Mr. Cornelius, the then Editor, daringly reintroduced it. But *Hansard* is what it has always been called, and what it will always be called.

In 1909, when the Official Report undertook its tremendous task, there were ten reporters, soon increased to twelve. At one time in the last war the numbers fell to seven, but afterwards were raised to eighteen, of whom one was a woman. The department is paid by the House of Commons, and to-day consists of twenty-four persons, there being an Editor, an Assistant Editor, and two sub-editors, in addition to twenty reporters. The only proceedings of the House which the reporters do not record are those in Select and Private Bill Committees, which are handled by a private firm, Gurneys, which was first entrusted with this responsibility by the House in 1813.

In February 1949 Mr. Speaker Clifton Brown delivered a ruling on the responsibility and scope of the Official Report to an interested and amused House. The burden of his statement was simply that the "Official Report" was not the Official Report. "*Hansard* he said, "is the Official Report of Parliamentary Debates . . . It is a report by people who are officially appointed as part of the staff of the House of Commons. That is the extent of the official position of *Hansard*. There is no authoritative matter in its record."[1] The point of this ruling was to make clear the fact that the *Journals of the House*, referred to earlier in this chapter, are the official records of the House; and that *Hansard* is merely a report of speeches.

The *Hansard* reporters occupy the first bench in the Press Gallery above the Speaker's Chair, where they scribble endlessly in their note-books while the House is sitting. A "turn" in the gallery lasts for ten minutes, and there are always two reporters, one taking the verbatim account, and the other waiting for his "turn," and helping his colleague if the House is noisy and the task of specifying each Member is difficult. The reporter who is actually taking down

1 Parliamentary Debates, Vol. 461, Column 1347 (17th February, 1949).

what is being said cannot look up to discover the Member who suddenly interjects from an obscure back bench, and his colleague is noting down the sequence of Members who speak, to act as a further check. A reporter may have ten minutes of blazing uproar in the House, with the Speaker (whom he cannot see) delivering important rulings, and Members constantly interrupting, or he may be blessed with a "turn" in which a Member reads out from copious notes (which the reporter may later borrow) in a peaceful and friendly solitude.

After his "turn" is completed, the reporter goes up to the *Hansard* offices above the Chamber and dictates his notes to a typist. Messages are sent winging down to the Chamber. "Would Mr. X be so good as to send up a list of figures he quoted about mineral deposits in North Wales?" "Would Mr. Y kindly send up his quotation from *Paradise Lost?*" "Would Mrs. Z be so good as to send up her notes?" or even, "Would Mr. W. kindly come to the official reporters' office?" After all doubtful matters have been disposed of, the corrected typescript is sent by messenger to the Stationery Officer, where it is set and printed. There are no proof copies, but errors are surprisingly few in the daily *Hansard*. A weekly *Hansard* is also published, and any mistakes that might have crept in are corrected.

It must not be imagined that the reporters record exactly what is said in the House. Mannerisms, mistakes, the inevitable "ums" and "ahs" and all the rest are generously omitted, and the attempt of *Hansard* is to reproduce what the Member meant to say rather than the merciless details of how he said it. Of course, there can be no alteration, by reporters or Members, of genuine "howlers," only the removal of mannerisms and the correction of errors is permitted. But the most shambling, incoherent speech can be transformed by the kind hand of *Hansard* into something very impressive. But there is nothing that can be done for a Member who declares, as one once did, that "Our prestige is a double-edged sword. On one side it is going up, but on the other side it is going down!" or, for the Minister who solemnly informed the House that "The agricultural policy of the Government is making progress in several fields!" or for the ex-Minister who recently informed the House that, "What might satisfy the Mohammedans would not appease the Moslems!" These gems are enshrined for ever in the august columns of the Official Report. "I hear a smile," an indignant Member once declared; "Have British troops to wait until they are murdered before they can use their weapons?" inquired another; "The law of supply and demand," another Member once loftily remarked, "will come along like a steam-roller and lead us on the road to ruin;" "I have no desire," a Member recently said, addressing the Speaker, "to question your partiality;" a Minister of Agriculture was once urged "to give a square deal to the hard-pressed beef producers in these lean times." *Hansard* itself is guilty of the occasional error. The Lord Advocate has been described as "the Lord's Abdicate," and the typescript report of a speech once read, "Whenever the Minister is attacked by the Opposition he appears to become a little violet!" These errors, rare and refreshing, add considerably to the gaiety of the House, but the amazing accuracy of the Report makes them very rare indeed. We have come a long way since Mr. Gladstone's maiden speech was described thus: "Mr. Gladstone made a few observations which were not audible in the Gallery."

There is no doubt that in gaining its accuracy, *Hansard* has lost much of its fun. An interruption is not mentioned unless the speaker refers to it, and it is only when a Member says angrily, "It is very easy for the Hon. Member to jeer," that *Hansard* acknowledges the presence of laughter. In the bad old days, *Hansard* once described a noisy scene in July 1880 thus:

SIR HENRY DRUMMOND WOLFF: . . . I am especially sorry at all to interfere with the equanimity of the Home Secretary (Sir William Harcourt). He occupies a very high position in this House—in the estimation of this House—but he occupies a far higher position in his own estimation. (*Cries of* "Oh! Oh!" *and* "Withdraw!") If hon. gentlemen opposite—(*Renewed cries of* "Withdraw!" "Order!" "Chair!" "Oh! Oh!") Will hon.

gentlemen—(*Cries again renewed, coupled with loud cries of* "Order!") . . .

To-day, none of these interruptions would be noted, as the Speaker did not refer to them, and in any event, if he had, they would have been recorded as *Interruption*. Furthermore, Wolff's lost sentence would have been recorded, since his assistance would have been sought afterwards by the reporter. It is interesting to compare this comparatively trivial scene in 1880 with the harsh exchanges in the House in the November of 1956 over the Suez crisis. It was difficult for a witness of the highly-charged and dramatic scene when the Speaker suspended the sitting on account of Grave Disorder, to recapture these passions when the day's *Hansard* appeared.

CAPTAIN PILKINGTON *rose*—

MR. BEVAN: I am on a point of order.

MR. SPEAKER: Order, order. I cannot have two Members on their feet at the same time. Would it not be possible for all these matters to be brought out in the course of the debate?[1]

HON. MEMBERS: No.

MR. SPEAKER: As I read the Motion, it is in the widest possible terms. All these matters could be raised.

HON. MEMBERS: No.

MR. BEVAN: They do not come within the Motion at all.

MR. SPEAKER: I think that the Motion—

HON. MEMBERS: No.

MR. GAITSKELL *rose*—

MR. SPEAKER: Order. The Motion is a general one.

HON. MEMBERS: No.

MR. SPEAKER: If the House will not listen to me——

HON. MEMBERS: No.

MR. SPEAKER: I will suspend the sitting. (*Interruption*) I have to inform the House that if it will not listen to me, I shall

---

1 This Motion, a Vote of Censure on the Government, was about to be debated. The uproar arose after Ministerial statements.

suspend the sitting. (Hon. Members: "Hear, hear.") That appears to some Hon. Members to be a desirable course. I am certainly not going to have the Chair put in the position of not being heard in this House of Commons. The sitting is suspended for half an hour.[1]

As factual reporting, this is unbelievably brilliant. Out of what appeared to be complete chaos, with furious interruptions from all corners of the House, a clear account of the exchanges, with their culmination, has been presented. But as a portrait of the scene in the House it is necessarily deficient. That is the responsibility of the newspapers, the Official Reporters argue; the task of *Hansard* is to give the Official Report, and although one may lament the passing of the vigorous and vivid *Hansard*, the accuracy and the impartiality of the modern Official Report are so important that in a final analysis it must be preferred. But it will be to the newspapers, and not to *Hansard*, that the future historians will turn in their endeavour to recapture the "mood of the House."

Every Member living in the London area will receive his copy of *Hansard* with his morning post every day after the House has met. In it he will read the complete account of the proceedings of the House up to 10.30 p.m. He will also probably receive the *Hansard* for the meetings of Standing Committees, if any have met on the previous day. *Hansard* is so accurate and so efficiently compiled that it tends to be taken for granted. It is only when the magnitude of the task confronting the reporters, editors, typists, and printers is remembered that their achievement can be realised. Members who speak quickly, mumble their words, swing away from microphones, speak in a babel of conversation or in a mælstrom of interruptions, are all amazingly recorded. And when even *Hansard* errs, the mistakes are accepted cheerfully by Members, particularly when they result in a Member apparently proudly declaring that, "I am, thank God, Mr. Speaker, able to put satin (Satan) behind me."

---

1 Parliamentary Debates, 5th Series, Vol. 558, Column 1625 (1st November, 1956).

CHAPTER EIGHT

Committee Work

"I found myself judging some confounded Scotch Water Bill . . .
Ten hours in an office would be preferable to the five I spent in
a crowded room over this dry Scotch Bill. No more Committees
for me!"

David Lloyd George, 1890[1]

The House of Commons has remained remarkably immune from
the modern tendency in most spheres of Government to delegate
almost everything to Committees. Any Committee set up by the
House is the creature of the House, and its recommendations can
be debated, accepted, rejected or ignored if the House so wishes.
A Bill sent to a Standing Committee has to return to the House;
a Report from a Select Committee merely contains suggestions;
with the solitary exception of the Kitchen Committee—to which
reference will be made later—no Select Committee has any powers
beyond making recommendations. The House appoints the
Committee and sets out its terms of reference, which the Committee
must adhere to, and which only the House can alter.

It is necessary to distinguish the several types of Committee
which function in the House. First, and most important of all,
there is the *Committee of the Whole House*, when the Speaker
leaves the Chair, the Chairman of Ways and Means or a member

---

1 Quoted on page 62 of Mr. Frank Owen's *Tempestuous Journey; The Life and Times of Lloyd George.*

of the Chairman's Panel controls the proceedings from the chair of the Clerk of the House, and the Mace is put "under the Table" on hooks provided for this purpose. It is thought that the House originally adopted this procedure to get rid of the presence of the Speaker in the Chair in the days when he was a Royal nominee, but one practical result of the procedure is that there is no limit on the number of times a Member may speak on one Question, and in discussions upon the details of legislation or finance this is extremely important.

When does the House go into Committee? First, there is the ordinary committee stage of a Bill, when the House has committed the measure to "a Committee of the Whole House" as opposed to a Standing Committee. Then there are the occasions when certain Bills have Financial Resolutions. These Resolutions are necessary when any Bill entails the expenditure of public money, and must be passed by the House after Second Reading before the Bill goes into Committee. The Resolution must be on the Order Paper, so that the House may inspect it in advance. At the appropriate moment after Second Reading, the Speaker inquires if the Resolution has received the approval of the Queen, and a Minister (usually signifying the fact by bowing towards the Chair) informs the House that it has. The Speaker then leaves the Chair, the Mace is put "under the Table" by the Serjeant at Arms, and the House becomes a Committee, in which Members may speak as often as they wish, although they are severely restricted in moving any Amendments, and the debate cannot last longer than forty-five minutes. It normally takes only a few seconds, and when the House has agreed to the Report from the Committee, the next stage of the Bill may begin.

Then there is the *Committee of Supply*. This is when the House resolves itself into a Committee to consider the details of the money to be spent by the Government on public services, such as Defence and the Civil Service. In fact this procedure is usually employed to initiate debates on matters of policy, and twenty-six Supply Days are set aside every year. The Opposition has the right of choosing the subject for debate on these "allotted days," and this is one of their most cherished privileges. Thus, if the Opposition think that the Minister of Housing is doing a bad job in not building enough houses, they can select the Ministry of Housing Vote from the Civil Estimates for discussion, and if they feel that the Minister has not made an adequate reply, they can move to reduce his salary by a token sum (usually £100). This is equivalent to a Vote of Censure, and, if carried, the Minister—and possibly the Government—would resign. The actual examination of the Estimates is nowadays hardly ever done in Committee of Supply; the procedure has become an opportunity for the Opposition to initiate a debate on any subject it wants. The rights of the Government are safeguarded, for they will get the money necessary for the running of the country on the last but one Supply Day. All "Votes" not passed by then are put from the Chair at half past nine, and no debate is permitted, although it is possible to force a division against any Vote. What happens in practice is that at nine-thirty on the last Supply Day the Chairman interrupts the business, and puts the Question on each Vote until all the money not previously voted has been agreed to by the House.

The *Committee of Ways and Means*, like the Committee of Supply, is set up by the House at the beginning of the Session, and its functions are to vote money from the Consolidated Fund to meet the expenditure agreed to by the Committee of Supply, and to authorise taxation. The Finance Bill is founded upon Resolutions of the Committee of Ways and Means, and it is to this Committee that the Chancellor of the Exchequer announces his Budget proposals in April.

These Committees are in fact merely the House of Commons sitting without the Speaker in the Chair, and with (in theory) less restricted rules of debate. When people talk of "Committees of the House of Commons" they are almost invariably referring to *Select Committees*, which are small Committees set up by the House for certain definite purposes. The work of *Standing Committees*, which examine Bills at their committee stage, has been described in Chapter Six.

The phrase "Select Committee" merely means a Committee of

Members selected by the House to do a particular job, and the procedure has been employed by the House for over three hundred years. The Select Committee is instructed to do work for which the House itself is not fitted, even if it had the time; it can examine witnesses—if it has the power to send for "persons, papers and records"—sifts evidence presented to it, and draws up a list of recommendations for the House. Having done this, the Committee has reached the limits of its powers, and it is up to the House to take what action it thinks fit.

Select Committees can be conveniently divided into three types, those appointed by the House to examine specific matters which arise in the course of the Session, those set up by Standing Order (such as the Public Accounts and Estimates Committees), and those normally set up at the beginning of each Session, of which the Selection and Kitchen Committees are examples. The House gives each Committee its terms of reference and appoints its Members, and it is not until this Resolution is passed by the House that the Committee can begin its work.

The first meeting of the Committee is called by the senior Member, and at this meeting the Chairman is chosen. He has no powers comparable to those of the Chairman of Ways and Means or of the Chairman of a Standing Committee; his authority depends almost entirely upon his personality and powers of persuasion. He is assisted by a Clerk from the Committee Office, who conducts the correspondence of the Committee, makes arrangements for witnesses, advises on procedural matters, and although he is not expected to be an expert on the subject under discussion—except, perhaps, in the case of the Committee of Privileges—he should be in a position to assist the Committee in its inquiry. Liaison Officers may be appointed by the appropriate Government Departments to help him and the Committee on complicated matters.

At its first meeting in one of the Committee Rooms, there is a general discussion about the Committee's provisional programme, and the best means of conducting the business allocated to it by the House. The Chairman probably outlines his ideas and invites other points of view. Let us suppose that the Committee has been set up to examine the accommodation facilities for Members in the Palace of Westminster. At the first meeting the Chairman says that he intends to ask the Serjeant at Arms and the Librarian to submit Memoranda giving the details of the department under the Serjeant, and of the Library—how many books are borrowed annually, the size of the staff, etc., etc.—and then to summon them to give evidence after the Memoranda have been examined. Another Member suggests that they should examine the Ministry of Works at some stage, the Clerk of the House, and the Speaker. The atmosphere when a Select Committee is deliberating is quite informal; the meeting is strictly private, there are few rules of procedure, Members can smoke, the discussion is more in the nature of a conversation than a debate, and the Clerk may be asked for his advice.

But when the Committee meets to take evidence the atmosphere is quite different. The Members sit round a horseshoe-shaped table, the Chairman sitting in the middle, facing the witnesses, with the Clerk beside him; between the Committee and the witness a shorthand writer records a verbatim report of the proceedings. Before the witnesses are actually summoned into the room the Chairman usually tells his colleagues of the general lines of the questions he intends to ask the witness, and there may be a brief discussion. The Clerk then calls in the witnesses, who have been nervously lurking in the corridor, the shorthand writer takes his place, and the Committee commences its labours. The verbatim Minutes of Evidence would read something like this:

Mr. Jones, C.B., Ministry of——, called in and examined.
Chairman

1. Mr. Jones, we are very much obliged to you for coming today, and for submitting such a helpful and detailed Memorandum. I should like to ask you, first of all, how long you have held your post at the Ministry?—I have been at the Ministry for nearly twelve years, and have held my present position for just under five years.

Mr. Greigson

2. I am sorry to interrupt, but might I ask what Mr. Jones's present position is?—I am Chief Establishment Officer.

The Chairman

3. How many people do you control?—Approximately ten thousand, excluding cleaners.

And so the examination continues, until the Committee feels that it has obtained all the necessary information from this and other witnesses. At the end of the Inquiry the Clerk prepares a Draft Report for the Chairman, which is usually drawn up after lengthy discussions with his Chairman. The general rule is that conclusions and controversial comments should be based on the evidence, which is published with the Report. Thus, if the Report says that "Your Committee are surprised to learn that the Chief Establishment Officer at the Ministry had only been in the Ministry for seven years before he took his present appointment, and recommend that more senior officials with greater experience should be appointed," there must be a reference to the appropriate Question and Answer, which in this case would be marked (Q. 1–3).

The Committee then considers this Draft Report, paragraph by paragraph, and when it has been approved, the Clerk goes to the Table of the House with a special form announcing the fact. This is minuted by the Clerks, and appears in the *Votes and Proceedings* for that day. The House orders the Report and the Minutes of Evidence to be printed, and the Clerk to the Committee is responsible for this. There can be no "minority report" from a Select Committee; the only manner in which individual Members can reveal that they objected to the Report is by moving Amendments which are defeated; these are then recorded in the Minutes of the Committee, which are published with the Report.

Having completed its labours, the Committee dies if it is one which has been appointed for a specific purpose, and it has no guarantee that the House will even debate its Report, let alone accept the advice which it contains.

Select Committees are noticeable for their impartiality and friendliness; it is rare for divisions to be taken on party lines, and most unusual for there to be any acrimony in discussion. Some Committees—particularly the Estimates sub-committees—travel to take evidence and inspect Government Departments, and these journeys help to increase the friendliness and non-partisanship which are of the greatest importance in detailed inquiries of this kind.

Having seen, in broadest terms, how a Select Committee works, let us look at some of the regular Select Committees which the House sets up.

COMMITTEE OF PRIVILEGES

This Committee is appointed by the House at the beginning of each Session, and usually consists of ten senior Members of the House, including the Leader of the House (who usually acts as Chairman), the Leader of the Opposition, and one of the Law Officers (either the Attorney-General or the Solicitor-General). It only meets when specific complaints of breach of privilege are referred to it by the House. The procedure is as follows. When an alleged breach of privilege is raised by a Member on the Floor of the House, the Speaker has to rule whether a *prima facie* case has been made out which will allow him to give the matter precedence over the Orders of the Day. If he does decide that an adequate case has been made, and rules thus, the Leader of the House moves that the matter complained of be referred to the Committee of Privileges. Even if the Speaker rules that there is no *prima facie* case, the House can still refer the matter to the Committee by carrying a Motion to this effect, but this must be taken on a following day, and not at the time when the Speaker makes his ruling. The Committee then examines the complaint, calls witnesses—which usually include the Clerk of the House—and reports back to the House. But even in the case of such a distinguished Committee, the House has been known to reject its recommendations.

COMMITTEE OF PUBLIC ACCOUNTS

This Committee was first set up in 1861 on a motion moved by Mr. Gladstone, and is one of the most active and responsible Committees which serve the House. Its principal task is to see that the money voted by Parliament has been spent in accordance with its wishes. The Comptroller and Auditor General, who has the status of an officer of the House, and has a large department to assist him in his task of auditing the nation's accounts, assists the Committee, and it is usually as a result of his reports that the Committee inquires into specific matters. For example, the Comptroller's department may discover than an aeroplane for the Royal Air Force cost a lot of money to build and was then found to be unsatisfactory, as the engines were too heavy, or had some other defect. The work of taking the engines out and putting new ones in cost more money. The Committee would summon the permanent officials of the Ministry of Aviation and the Air Ministry, and inquire about what went wrong. If the Committee decides that there has been waste and inefficiency, it reports accordingly to the House. In recent years these Reports have had considerable publicity, and the Committee's work acts as a powerful check upon incompetent forecasting of expenditure. Although it principally deals with wastage which has occurred, its Reports can be as a salutary shock to departments, so that they act more carefully in the future.

THE ESTIMATES COMMITTEE

Whereas the Public Accounts Committee looks at public money after it has been spent, the Estimates Committee concentrates upon current expenditure. The Committee was first set up in 1912, but it was only since the last war that it has assumed any real importance. At the moment the Committee consists of 43 Members (until 1960 it numbered 36) and these are divided into Sub-Committees, numbered B, C, D, etc., each of which takes a particular aspect of government expenditure and inquires into it. Sub-Committee A consists of the Chairmen of the Sub-Committees, and it is this body which decides which subjects should be examined and which Members should serve on each Sub-Committee. In 1959–60, for example, the subjects chosen were the Central Office of Information, the Headquarters Organisation of the Royal Navy, the Board of Trade, the Commonwealth Relations Office, and Ancient Monuments maintained and managed by the Ministry of Works. The Inquiries usually begin in January, and the Sub-Committee reports to the full Committee in June or July; the full Committee can in theory reject the Report from any of its Sub-Committees, but in fact it usually confines itself to minor alterations. The Reports are published one by one as Reports from the full Committee, and usually attract considerable public interest. The result of the excellent work which the Committee has done in recent years is that it has been increased in size and in its terms of reference, and has emerged from a position of relative obscurity to one of influence in the control of public money by the House of Commons. It can only *recommend* certain economies, but these recommendations can carry great weight with Ministers and departments, who are obliged to reply to them, and these replies are published.

Although the Committee is not very popular with certain Ministries—and it is undeniable that some of its Reports have been controversial—it has great importance, if only as "nuisance value," to keep officials on their toes. Also, officials who live with complicated problems of administration tend to become so obsessed with the details that they lose sight of fundamental facts which immediately strike a Committee of laymen examining the problem with a fresh mind. For example, when a Sub-Committee inquired into the Reserve Fleet in 1955–6, they discovered that no one in the Admiralty knew how much H.M.S. *Vanguard*—a battleship which had lain in reserve for many years—cost to maintain. They recommended that more attention should be paid to costing matters of this kind, and as a result the Admiralty overhauled its Costing Section to improve this side of its organisation. This is one tiny example of how the Estimates Committee can draw the attention of Government Departments to weaknesses in their organisation which can cause a waste of public money.

COMMITTEE ON NATIONALISED INDUSTRIES

This is a new Committee, which has risen very quickly in importance in the past five years. Its task is to look at the financial state of health of the nationalised industries—the two Air Corporations (B.O.A.C. and B.E.A.) and British Railways have been the subjects of Reports in the past two years—and to make observations on them. At the moment this is one of the very few ways in which the Commons can keep a check on these industries, since there is no Minister who can answer for the day-to-day management of these enormous concerns.

COMMITTEE ON STATUTORY INSTRUMENTS

Many Acts of Parliament give powers to Ministers or the Queen in Council which they can exercise by means of Statutory Instruments, which in effect are regulations. If the Instrument is liable to Parliamentary action, the Act will specify whether it has to be *approved* by Parliament—in which case the Instrument may be debated—or if it will automatically become law after it has been "laid on the Table" for a period and the fact recorded in the *Votes and Proceedings*. The only way for the House to kill an Instrument of the second type is to pass a "prayer" to the Queen to annul it. A great number of these Instruments are laid on the Table each year, and only comparatively few are ever debated. The task of the Committee—which has the legal assistance of the Speaker's Counsel—is to scrutinise those Instruments which are subject to proceedings in either House and to report to the House on any exceptional matter which they discover. This marks the limits of the powers of this Committee.

THE KITCHEN COMMITTEE

The Select Committee on Kitchen and Refreshment Rooms (House of Commons) is of even greater antiquity than the Public Accounts Committee, having been appointed for the first time in 1848. Its duties are confined to the management of the refreshment rooms of the House, which serve Members, Officers of the House, and Strangers. It is unique among Committees of the House in that it can actually do things rather than merely make recommendations. It consists of thirteen Members, and appoints three Sub-Committees to deal with Buying, Staff, and Wine matters. The Manager of the Refreshment Department is appointed by the Committee, and attends meetings by invitation, and works closely with the Chairman in the day-to-day running of the Department.

The Committee usually meets once a month when the House is sitting, and examines the monthly accounts and discusses problems which have arisen. Although it has power to send for persons, papers and records, it very rarely summons witnesses, and its meetings are extremely informal, although a Clerk from the Committee Office is present to record the Minutes. The Committee usually meets in one of the small dining-rooms on the Terrace Level, and, by a curious coincidence, at tea-time. Members sit on either side of a long table, and the proceedings resemble those of a meeting of company directors rather than that of a Committee of the House. It usually publishes only one Report a year, when it informs the House of its financial position. For several years after the war the Department made a heavy loss, which led to numerous critical articles in the newspapers about the taxpayer subsidising M.P.s' food, but as a result of a determined endeavour to reduce costs, the Department now breaks even, and even makes a small profit.

Members can put down Questions for oral or written answer in the House to the Chairman of the Kitchen Committee, but in the normal course of events complaints are sent privately to him, the Manager, or his colleagues on the Committee, and are dealt with in this manner. In spite of the venerable antiquity of the Kitchen Committee, there is a school of thought which believes that its functions could be done with equal efficiency by an informal Committee, set up by the Speaker, as is done in the case of the Library.

COMMITTEE OF SELECTION

The Committee of Selection is responsible for choosing Members to serve on Standing Committees, Private Bill Committees, and some Joint Committees of Lords and Commons, when it appoints the Commons' representatives. It meets—and the tradition is a hallowed one—on Wednesdays when there is business to transact at 3.15 p.m., in Committee Room 13, under the eye of the bust of Sir John Mowbray, a distinguished and unremembered Chairman of the 1880's. The Clerk to the Committee prepares a detailed list of the Bills referred to Standing Committees and Private Bill Committees, with the names of those Members whose names are on the backs of the Bills as official supporters, and those who spoke in the Second Reading debate. The Clerk is also responsible for working out the party proportions, so that the Government will have its appropriate majority. If Members particularly wish to serve on a certain Committee they can mention the fact either to the Whips or to the Chairman of the Committee, who will see what he can do. It must be admitted, however, that applications for *not* being on a Standing Committee are rather more common. In the case of exceedingly dreary and protracted Bills it has been darkly suggested by some Members that the Whips had drawn up a list of supporters against whom they had a particular grudge and had appointed them to the Committee, but this has always been indignantly denied.

When the Committee has selected the Members to serve on a particular Committee, the Clerk informs these Members by card of their appointment, and a Report appears in the *Votes and Proceedings*. Once a Committee has started to meet, no Member can be taken off except for a particularly good reason.

These are only a few of the Committees which are set up by the House to do detailed work for which the House is not fitted, and although there are several others of considerable importance and usefulness, those I have mentioned in detail are the most important. Committee work can be extremely dull for Members and officials, and there is usually no political advantage whatever to be gained from conscientious service in this field. It is probably for this very reason that some of the most gifted and public-spirited Members regularly serve on Committees, regarding the duty as one of the less rewarding but more important aspects of their public responsibilities.

*Suggestions for Further Reading
and a Short Glossary of
Parliamentary Terms*

Suggestions for Further Reading

This list of books is set out so that the reader may progress from the more simple books on the subject to the more complicated by easy stages. There are more unsatisfactory books written on the House of Commons than on almost any other single subject, and each of the books mentioned below is confidently recommended as exceptions to the general rule. There are other good books on the subject, but this list contains one of each type so that there need be no overlapping.

Parliament Past and Present (1904) (Two Volumes)
A lavishly illustrated history of Parliament, now out of print, but obtainable from any good library.

LUCY, SIR HENRY: *Peeps at Parliament* (1903) and *Later Peeps at Parliament* (1905)
Both these books, also out of print but obtainable from good libraries, are full of good Parliamentary stories and are excellently illustrated. Lucy was the Parliamentary correspondent for *Punch* and *The Strand Magazine* for many years, and no one has ever written more amusingly and shrewdly about the everyday life of the House of Commons.

COCKS, T. G. B.: *The Parliament at Westminster* (Edward Arnold,1948)
This is a good introduction for younger children, and although it

is now out of date in some respects, it is recommended for children of the 12–14 age group.

ILBERT, SIR GOURTNEY: *Parliament* (Home University Library: Oxford University Press, Revised Edition, 1947)
A graceful, concise, and authoritative study of Parliament; probably the most satisfactory short book on the subject.

MACKENZIE, KENNETH: *The English Parliament* (Pelican Books, 1951)
A brief history of Parliament, written simply and clearly, and recommended as an admirable introduction to the subject.

JENNINGS, SIR IVOR: *Parliament* (Cambridge University Press, Revised Edition, 1958)
An interesting, vivid, and well-written portrait of Parliament. It suffers from the disadvantage that the author has had no personal experience of Parliamentary life.

NICOLSON, NIGEL: *People and Parliament* (Weidenfeld & Nicolson, 1958)
Mr. Nicolson was Conservative Member for Bournemouth East from 1952 to 1959, when, after a heated controversy with the local Conservative Association over his attitude to capital punishment and the Suez Crisis, he retired from being the candidate. A large part of the book is devoted to this subject, but there are some excellent chapters on the House of Commons. Unlike many books written by Members or ex-Members, this is a sensible, accurate and illuminating portrait of the House of Commons to-day.

TAYLOR, ERIC: *The House of Commons at Work* (Pelican Books, Revised Edition, 1959)
This is the only reasonably brief and clear introduction to the extremely complicated subject of the procedure of the House.

MORRISON, HERBERT (now Lord Morrison of Lambeth):

Government and Parliament; A Survey from the Inside (Oxford University Press, Revised Edition, 1959)
Lord Morrison has been a leading personality in the House of Commons for twenty-five years, and became Leader of the House and Foreign Secretary in the 1945–51 Labour Government. His book is recommended as an interesting and refreshingly clear account of the machinery of Government, and embraces the work of the Cabinet, Civil Service, and House of Lords as well as that of the House of Commons.

ABRAHAM, L. A., AND HAWTREY, S. C.: *A Parliamentary Dictionary* (Butterworth, 1956)
Good for reference purposes.

CAMPION, LORD: *An Introduction to the Procedure of the House of Commons* (Third Edition, Macmillan, 1958)
Lord Campion was Clerk of the House for many years, and the most recent edition of his book has been extensively revised in the light of modern changes in procedure. It is not happily titled, for it is a detailed and authoritative book of reference, recommended only for very advanced students, and then only for reference purposes.

Among autobiographies or biographies of distinguished Members, the following are particularly recommended.

HERBERT, SIR ALAN: *Independent Member* (Methuen, 1950)
Sir Alan Herbert was Independent Member for Oxford University from 1936 to 1950. Although much of this amusing book is autobiographical, one chapter entitled "The Torture Chamber" is particularly recommended as a sardonic but accurate description of the tribulations of a private Member.

DISRAELI, BENJAMIN: *Life of Lord George Bentinck* (1851)
The most brilliantly written political biography in the English

language, written by a man who had played a leading part in Bentinck's career, and who later became Prime Minister twice. It is a short book, but contains some wonderfully vivid descriptions of great Parliamentary occasions.

CHURCHILL, (SIR) WINSTON SPENCER: *Lord Randolph Churchill* (One volume edition, Odhams, 1951)
Lord Randolph Churchill achieved an astonishing Parliamentary reputation in five years of active politics. Sir Winston's biography of his father, first published in 1905, contains weaknesses as a portrait of a man, but is magnificent as a portrait of the House of Commons in the 1880's.

WINTERTON, LORD: *Orders of the Day* (Cassell, 1953)
Lord Winterton was "Baby" of the House when he was first elected in 1904, and retired as "Father" of the House in 1951. His reminiscences of the House over that long period contain many excellent Parliamentary stories and portraits of leading political figures.

GRANT, JAMES: *Random Recollections of the House of Commons* (1836)
Long out of print, this delightful book is the best portrait of the old House of Commons, and is recommended to senior students.

A Short Glossary of Parliamentary Terms

This Glossary only includes the more common Parliamentary terms. In the case of those which have been explained already in the text, reference is made to the appropriate pages.

ADJOURNMENT OF THE HOUSE. When a motion "That this House do now adjourn" is carried, or the House is adjourned by the Speaker pursuant to the Standing Orders or for some other reason, it stands adjourned till the following sitting day, unless the motion has specifically stated when the House will reassemble. The motion is often used when the House wishes to have a general debate on a subject—such as Foreign Affairs—without being limited by a particular motion. The House has adjourned as a mark of respect on the death of a distinguished Member or ex-Member.

"BABY" OF THE HOUSE. The youngest Member of the House of Commons.

BACK-BENCHER. Any Member who is not in the Government or in the inner councils of the Opposition.

BAR OF THE HOUSE. See page 22.

BILL, PRIVATE. See pages 102–8.

BILL, PUBLIC. See pages 81–102.

BUDGET. The proposals for raising revenue for the public service made by the Chancellor of the Exchequer to the Committee of Ways and Means soon after the opening of each financial year (1st April), in a statement in which he also reviews the condition of the public income and expenditure. *See also*, pages 1–2.

CLOSURE. This is the procedure by which debate can be brought to an end although some Members wish to continue it. A Motion "That the Question be now put" can be moved by any Member at any time, but it is up to the Speaker (or the Chairman of Ways and Means if the House is in Committee) to decide if the motion is justified. If he decides that it is, the Question "That the Question be now put" is put at once, and cannot be debated; a hundred Members must support the motion, or it is declared to be not carried, even though there may be a majority for the Closure. If the motion is carried, the original Question before the House is put at once. The same rules apply to the acceptance of the Closure by the Chairman of a Standing Committee, with the exception of the fact that a quorum of the Committee must vote in favour of the motion.

CONSOLIDATED FUND. See pages 1–2.

COUNT. See pages 44 and 66, also "Quorum" below.

DEBATE. This may only take place in the House when a Motion has been moved and the appropriate Question ("That the Bill be now read a second time," etc.) has been proposed from the Chair. *See also*, page 89.

DISSOLUTION. See page 23.

DIVISION. See pages 89–92.

"FATHER" OF THE HOUSE. The Member who has sat in the House without a break for the longest period, and not necessarily the oldest Member.

FINANCE BILL. This is introduced after every Budget to give legislative effect to the proposals presented to the Committee of Ways and Means by the Chancellor of the Exchequer. It is a Bill to impose or change taxation, and is "founded" upon resolutions from the Committee of Ways and Means. *See also*, page 1.

GANGWAY. The benches of the House are divided on each side into two sections by a gangway. Members who sit "below the Gangway" in the part of the House farther from the Speaker are recognised as having a greater degree of independence from the party point of view than those who regularly sit "above the Gangway.".

MOTION. Basically, a Motion is a proposal made to the House by a Member which, if agreed to, will purport to express the judgment or will of the House.

OBSTRUCTION. This process, popularly known in America as "filibustering", consists of a Member or group of Members speaking at great length and using other stratagems to delay the business of the House. The modern rules of the House—particularly the Closure (see above)—are designed to discourage this practice, but it cannot be entirely eliminated, as the right of the Commons to complete freedom of speech is necessarily threatened by too severe rules against speeches, and it is felt that the rights of a Member or group of Members to oppose and delay business which they dislike or feel would be harmful to the country should not be unduly restricted.

ORDER PAPER. This consists of a number of papers published each morning under the authority of the Speaker and compiled by the Clerks in conjunction with the Government Whips, and which give details of forthcoming business for the House.

ORDERS OF THE DAY. Any business which has been appointed by order of the House for consideration on a particular day, and printed by direction of the Government in the order which they decide except on those days specifically reserved for Private (i.e. back-bench) Members.

"PAIRING." See pages 43 and 46.

PETITIONS. See pages 68 and 103–6.

PRIVILEGE. See pages 73-4 and 126-7.

PROROGATION. When the Queen "prorogues" Parliament, which she does by means of Lords Commissioners, she brings that Session to an end and gives the date for the beginning of the next Session of Parliament. *See also*, footnote to page 23.

QUESTION, PROPOSING AND PUTTING THE. See page 89.

QUESTIONS TO MINISTERS. See pages 69–75.

QUORUM. The quorum of the House of Commons—the minimum number of Members who must be present in the Chamber—is forty, including the Speaker. The Speaker does not "count the House" to see if a quorum is present unless a Member calls his attention to the fact that there are less than forty Members present. If, at the end of four minutes, forty Members have not entered the Chamber, the House is adjourned. The House may not be counted between 7.30 p.m. and 8.30 p.m. on a normal sitting day, or between 1.15 p.m. and 2.15 p.m. on a Friday. *See also*, page 44. The Quorum of a *Standing Committee* varies with its size; for a large Committee—of forty-five Members, for example—it is fifteen. It is the duty of the Clerks to inform the Chairman when there is not a quorum present, upon which the proceedings are suspended until a quorum is present. The quorum of each *Select Committee* is fixed by the order of the House which sets up the Committee, and it cannot proceed to any business until a quorum is present. *See also*, page 66.

ROYAL ASSENT. See pages 97–9.

SESSION. See footnote to page 23.

STANDING ORDERS OF THE HOUSE OF COMMONS. See pages 63–4.

STRANGERS. House of Commons' description of visitors. Hence Strangers' Gallery. Strangers' Cafeteria, etc.

SUPPLY, Committee of. See pages 121–2.

TEN-MINUTE RULE. See page 101.

TEN O'CLOCK RULE. See page 78.

TREASURY BENCH. The front bench above the gangway on the right of the Speaker, reserved by courtesy for members of the Government.

WAYS AND MEANS. The Committee of Ways and Means has two functions; to authorise taxation, to vote money from the Consolidated Fund to meet expenditure agreed to by the Committee of Supply (see page 121). *See also*, BUDGET above, and page 122.

WHIPS. See pages 43–6.